KAARI UPSON

ΔΕΣΤΕ

DESTE Foundation for Contemporary Art

KAARI UPSON

2000 WORDS

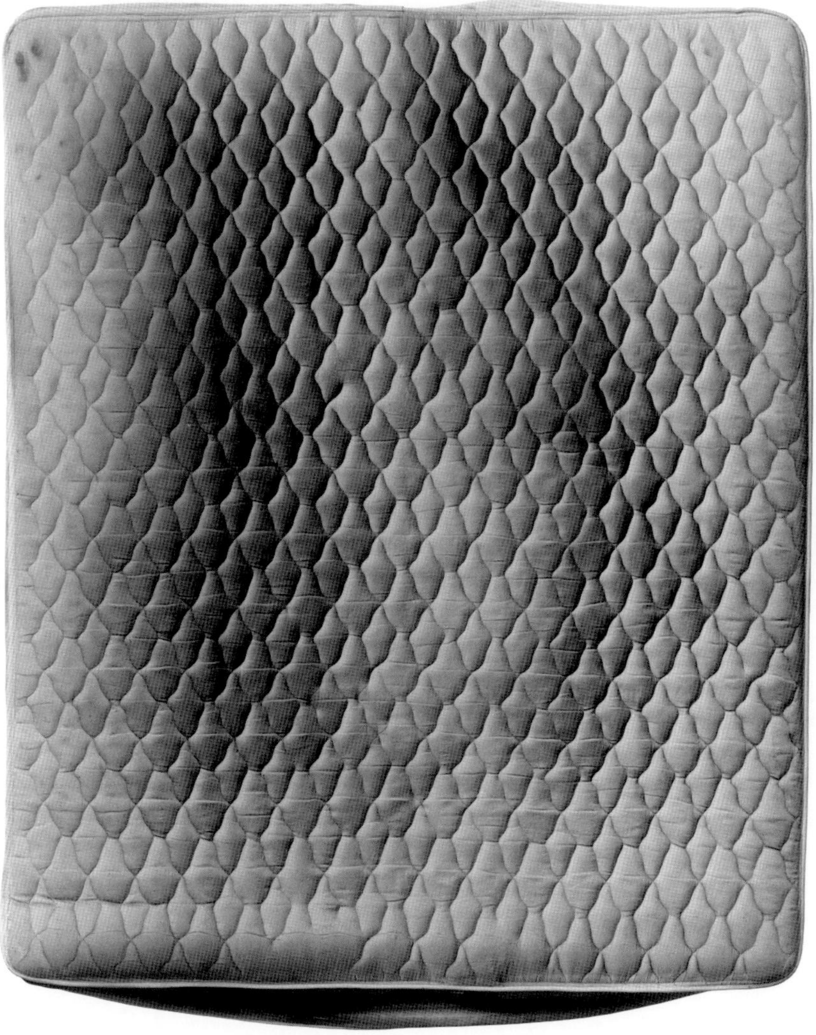

DOMESTIC DISTURBANCE

Ali Subotnick

Like a shaman, Kaari Upson imbues her work with a sort of mystical animism—the weight of a past life, a spirit or remnant of a lost soul. This transference of energy is present in every sculpture, painting, drawing, and video, which belong to chapters in an elaborate narrative woven from memory and conjecture, fact and fiction. Adopting strategies from anthropology and psychoanalysis, Upson believes that the key to accessing one's self is located in one's possessions, especially those contained in the home. These inanimate objects are infused with one's hopes, dreams, fears, and desires. Her pseudoscientific approach is largely intuitive and speculative, creating confounding, haunting works that feel both familiar and foreign.

Upson's investigations into the psyche began over ten years ago when a small fire granted her access to an abandoned McMansion across from her family home in San Bernardino, California. She had heard stories about the mysterious neighbor who once lived there and threw wild parties, but had never met him. Inside she found upended beds, boxes full of personal belongings, and ephemera that included journals in which her neighbor had transcribed his dreams, detailed his goals, and recounted his past for a memoir, along with real estate documents, contracts, photo albums, and snapshots. Upson set the materials aside and a few years later, when she was thinking about the implications of trespassing and profiling by examining someone's possessions, she began to sift through the boxes. She learned that her neighbor was into astrology and self-improvement, played tennis and Frisbee, and that he idolized Hugh Hefner, modelling his home on the Playboy Mansion. It was as if he wanted to create a satellite Playboy clubhouse in dismal San Bernardino. When she lost his dream journal, she was devastated, but it only deepened her curiosity about him. Recognizing the potential of that absence, she began to fill the holes—a recurring theme in her work—both literally and metaphorically.

Upson gave her neighbor an alias, Larry, and soon he developed into a multidimensional character distinct from the actual man who had lived in that house. She has told his story countless times and, like an urban myth or a game of telephone, it has morphed and developed so many tangents that even Upson struggles to distinguish fact from fiction. As she delved deeper, her own story began to merge with his, and with every new fact or piece of information, she gave herself license to expand her fantasies and conjecture about his story. As Upson explains, "The objective reality of the man I construct collapses into the subjective fiction I create, until they merge and I am more him than he is."[1] Larry became her obsession, her nemesis, her muse. She used him as a stand-in to analyze her relationships with the men in her life: her father, who is the same age as Larry; brother; first crush; husband; lovers; etc.

A series of works developed out of the narrative, which Upson calls "The Larry Project" (2007–ongoing). When a second fire destroyed his house completely, Upson, with the help of her father, captured it on video. Later, she made *It's Never Enough* (2008), a scorched table with these words carved into it so that they could be read in the shadow the table makes on the floor below. She also made a series of diptychs, *Untitled (Kiss)* (2008, pp. 20–21) and *Kiss Skinned 1* (2009, pp. 22–23), based on a self-portrait and a portrait of Larry. While the paint was still wet, she pressed the two faces—hers and Larry's—together multiple times, creating distorted, often grotesque images—the two becoming one. Sometimes she used thick and goopy paint, other times thin and sinewy;

sometimes she smashed the portraits together once or twice, other times six or seven times; sometimes the pressure was heavy, other times, light. She pushed the series to the limit, until she felt like she had exhausted the process through persistence and repetition, a recurring method in her practice. In the end her *Kiss* paintings not only merged Larry with Upson; they also illustrate how one can lose oneself in a relationship and how relationships can distort one's self-awareness.

Upson's obsession with Larry continued to deepen. Inspired by the life-size doll that Oskar Kokoschka commissioned of his former lover Alma Mahler, Upson created a life-size Larry doll. Instead of giving the doll Larry's brown eyes, it has blue eyes like her father and Robby Benson, her teenage crush, who bears a stark resemblance to Larry; her previous infatuation for Benson encouraged her fascination with Larry. To represent the honeymoon phase of their "relationship," Upson created a series of photographs of herself with the doll in intimate scenarios (*The Larry Project Chapter Two: Honeymoon Period*, 2007). But all honeymoons come to an end. Not unlike Kokoschka, who beheaded and destroyed his Mahler doll at a party, Upson cut the Larry doll up. In the first of a series of videos for "The Larry Project" (*As Long as It Takes–Part I: The Head*, 2007), Upson, dressed in white overalls and wearing a gingham surgical mask, straddles the Larry doll and excitedly recounts everything she knows about Larry while she carefully decapitates and skins him, and subsequently puts his head over her own.

For the next chapter in her story about Larry, Upson constructed a replica of the iconic Playboy Mansion Grotto (*The Grotto*, 2008–2009). The grotto became the site for an "exorcism" of sorts—an attempt to purge herself of Larry. In it, she projected videos of a new character she had created, her fictional twin Chrissie, who represents the created self (the woman) in relation to the merged self (the couple). The videos depict Upson and Chrissie participating in various sexual fantasies, as well as several actual recorded sessions of Upson consulting with an array of spiritual guides. These videos were visible only through cracks and peepholes in the grotto, turning unsuspecting viewers into voyeurs.

Returning her attention to Larry, Upson cast the doll in a wax-based charcoal—a material chosen for its impermanence—and eventually created a female counterpart for the Larry doll using a combination of its body parts, casts of her own body parts, and prosthetics. The resulting pair of broken figures, *Dismembered/Remembered (Charcoal Figures)* (2015, pp. 72–81), lies lifelessly in a heap of dismembered limbs, wigs, fingers, and shoes, melting into a black tablet on which they will sleep for eternity. This work shows how diligently Upson has explored the practice of creating objects through failure and repetition. It also demonstrates her desire to experiment with unorthodox techniques and work under extreme circumstances leading to unpredictable outcomes.

The same can be said of her series of smoke paintings (2009–2011), which were loosely inspired by the fires at Larry's house and created with an elaborate homemade apparatus that enabled Upson to catch smoke onto painted boards and mirrors. She also made a latex gate (*Balcony*, 2011) inspired by the gate at Larry's mansion, which was in turn inspired by the gates at the Playboy mansion, and latex crutches (*Cult of Invalidism*, 2012, pp. 28–37). The flaccid, dirty crutches, incapable of propping someone up, hang limply, uselessly, suggesting illness and codependency. Upson revisited Larry's house once again with *Mirrored Staircase Inversion* (2011–2012), a latex inversion of the grand double staircase that once led to his room. For this work, a hole in the form of the staircase was dug into the earth where the house once stood, and gallons of pink latex were poured into it. The resultant skin was then extracted in an endurance-testing private performance, and brought back to her studio. This and other similar acts take on a ritualistic significance for Upson, as she strives to purge herself of Larry's hold, while at the same time trying to reveal the mysteries embedded in his possessions.

Her interest in domestic objects continued and, flashing back to the upended beds she had found in Larry's house, Upson started collecting discarded mattresses found on the streets of Los Angeles. She developed a technique for casting them in a variety of materials including silicone, fiberglass, and urethane, which capture every detail of the original texture, stitching, and pattern. Each mold is destroyed in the process, so each cast is unique. Upson then painted them almost blindly, with only a vague idea of what she wanted to achieve, embracing a tremendous amount of unpredictability to transform the mattresses into unique artworks. As the title suggests, *Death Bed* (2015, pp. 100–03) is cast from a hospital bed that most likely witnessed a death or two. Painted with mystical greens, purples, and blues, it conveys an otherworldly presence. Likewise, *Crib Diptych* (2015, pp. 104–07) feels almost euphoric with its strange patterning, dents, stains, and wrinkles. In *226* (2013, pp. 42–45), which has a sagging bottom and circular imprints resembling bedsprings overlapping with a hastily painted grid, she inserted strange objects like soda cans in places they don't belong. These works represent an absence of the body, evoking loneliness, emptiness, and loss, but with their swirling, psychedelic colors, illusionistic shadows, and dizzying patterns, they become hallucinogenic vessels of memories and dreams.

After working with mattresses, Upson turned to couches and couch cushions. A specific circular couch design first attracted her attention for its communal, therapeutic quality, and because of its connection to the human body, specifically the anus. When she cast the seats, they became something entirely different from their original forms—deflated, flaccid, and inert like sagging butts, breasts, and bellies. These forms contrast with the vibrant colors and intoxicating shading Upson painted them with. *Left Brace*

Erase, Back Brace Face (2016, pp. 108–17) is one of her most ambitious furniture pieces yet: two sectional couches fold in on themselves, facing off in a sort of suspended duel. Upson also casts carpets, buckets, aloe vera plants, cinder blocks, and even doors. For the anthropomorphic *Door (closet)* (2014–2016, pp. 56–63), a standard closet door stands upright, supported with a bloated cast of a cinder block, but provides neither entrance nor exit. From the mattresses to seats and cushions, Upson has embraced the banal, domestic objects that we rely on every day. By exhausting the meanings and references imbued in these items, Upson finds new methods for creating compelling auratic objects.

Upson's most recent work is themed around her mother. Her mother's incessant habit of cracking open a can of Pepsi and declaring her satisfaction with an emphatic "Ahhhh" inspired Upson to create *Untitled (1000 cans)* (2015, pp. 82–87). These actual Pepsi cans are emptied of their sugary contents and filled with liquid aluminum, merging the liquid and the solid. Just as she transformed mattresses into mystical paintings and sculptures, Upson turns the ubiquitous American soda into a sacred relic. Amassed in an absurdly huge quantity, the cans represent the desire for consumption and possession, and her mother's wholehearted embrace of all things American.

From the bedroom to the living room to the kitchen, since the first trespass into Larry's McMansion, the idea of the house, its contents, and occupants have been continuous thread through Upson's work. What can one learn about someone by entering his or her home? What memories, fears, and desires remain in a house when the occupant has departed? These are some of the questions that drive Upson's continued investigations. Part Sherlock Holmes, part Dr. Frankenstein, with a tireless energy and drive to unravel and reveal meanings and motivations, Upson carries the same torch as Eva Hesse, Mike Kelley, Paul McCarthy, and Lynda Benglis. Yet she constantly invents her own language and processes for art-making and storytelling. Upson explains: "The challenge of defining the 'me' in this project is a final manifestation of the loss of perspective [that] it presents."[2] Who's to say which perception is right?

1 Kaari Upson, “The Larry Project” (Master of Fine Arts thesis, California Institute for the Arts, 2007), 1.

2 Ibid., 1.

WORKS

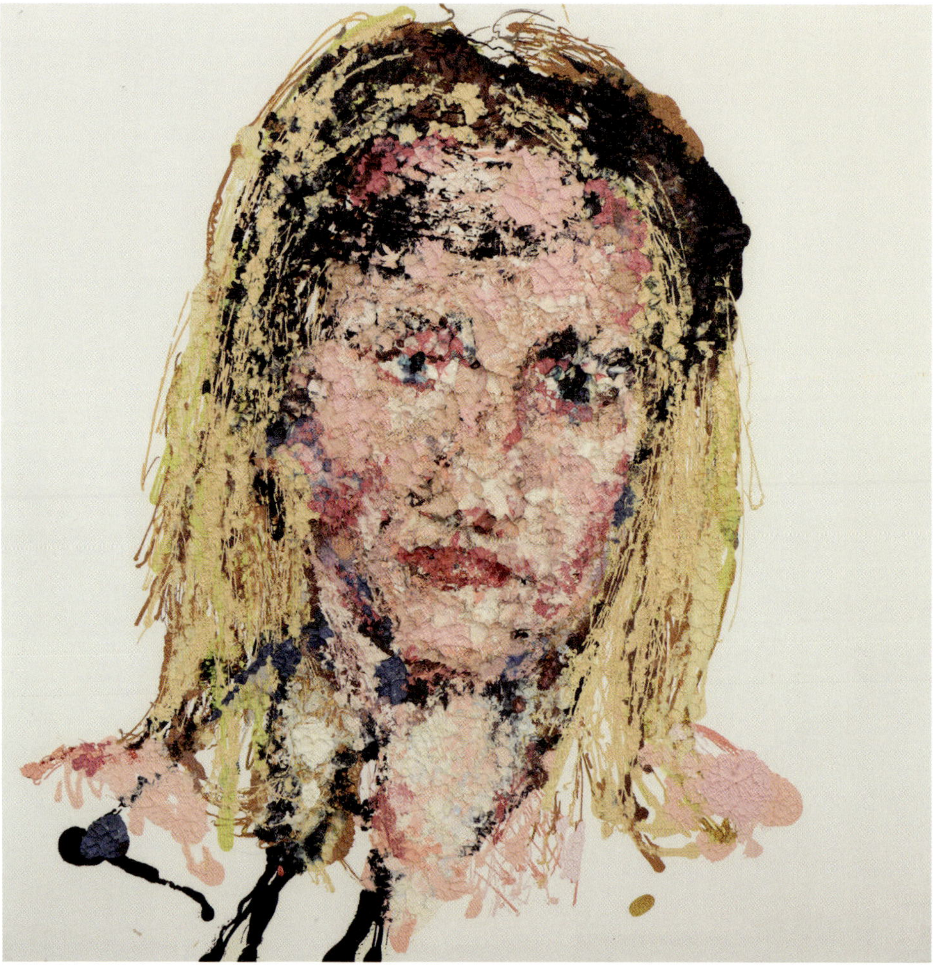

Untitled (Kiss), 2008

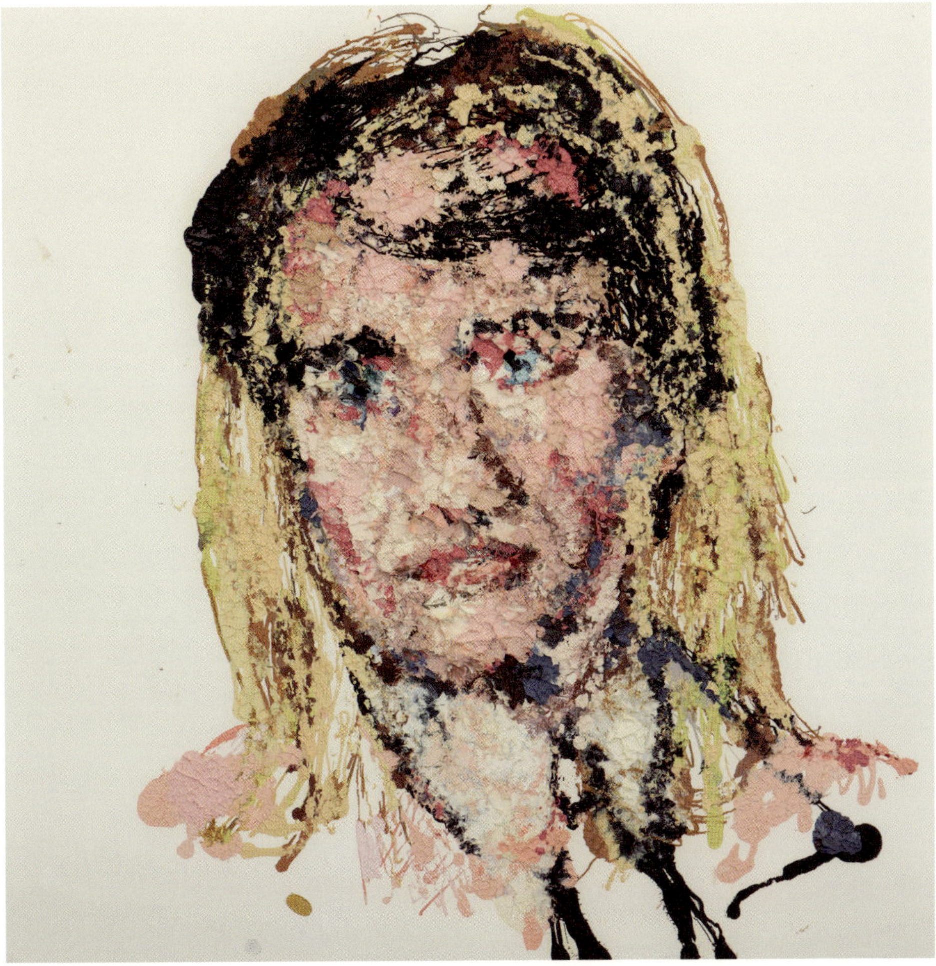

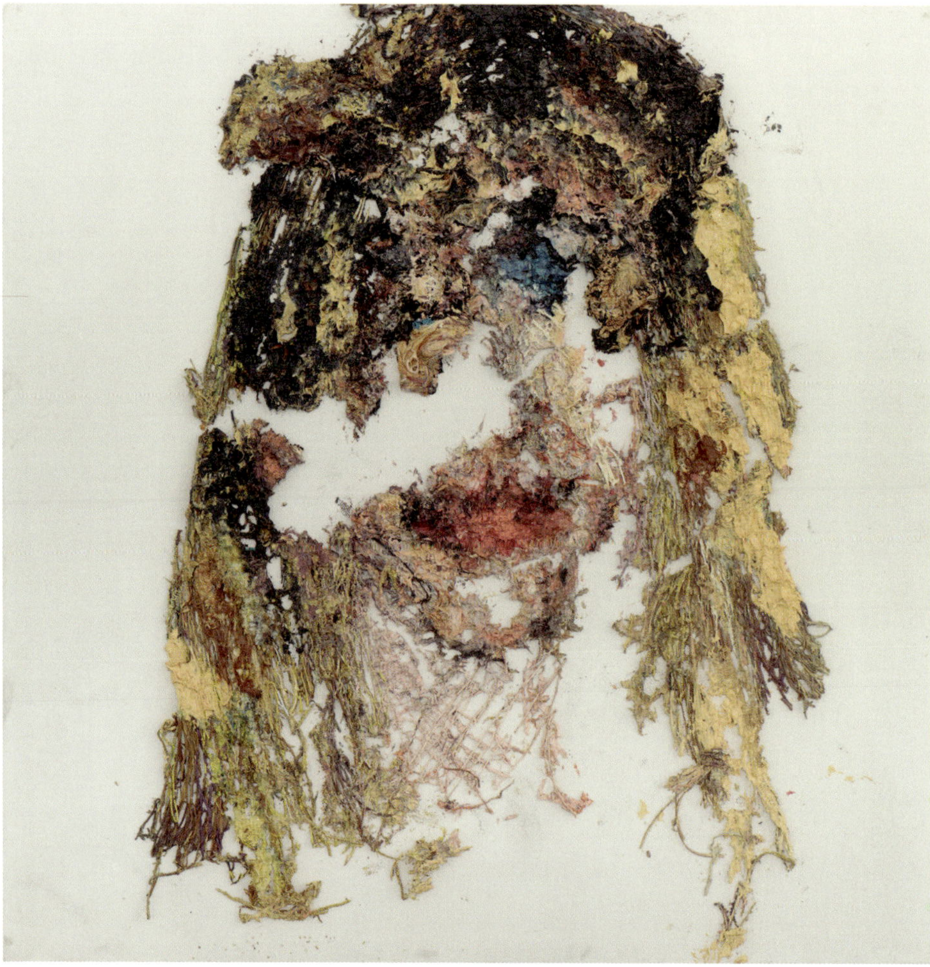

Kiss Skinned 1, 2009

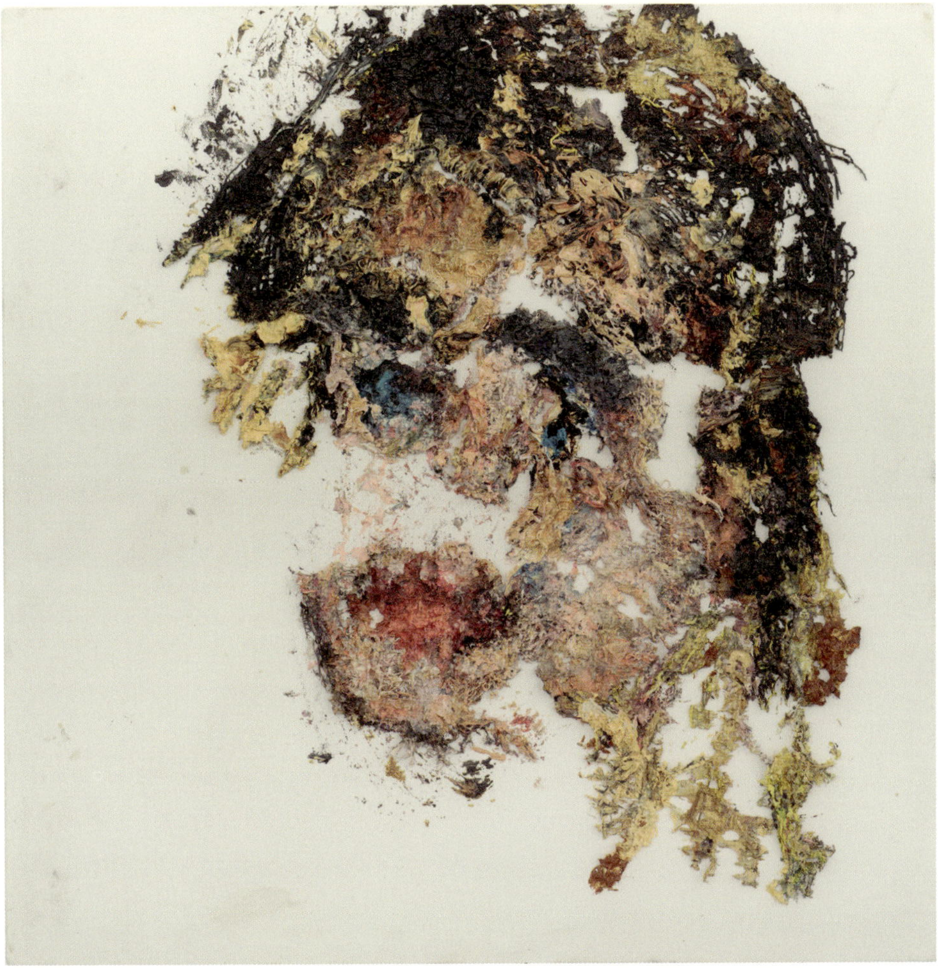

Event Horizon, 2011–2017

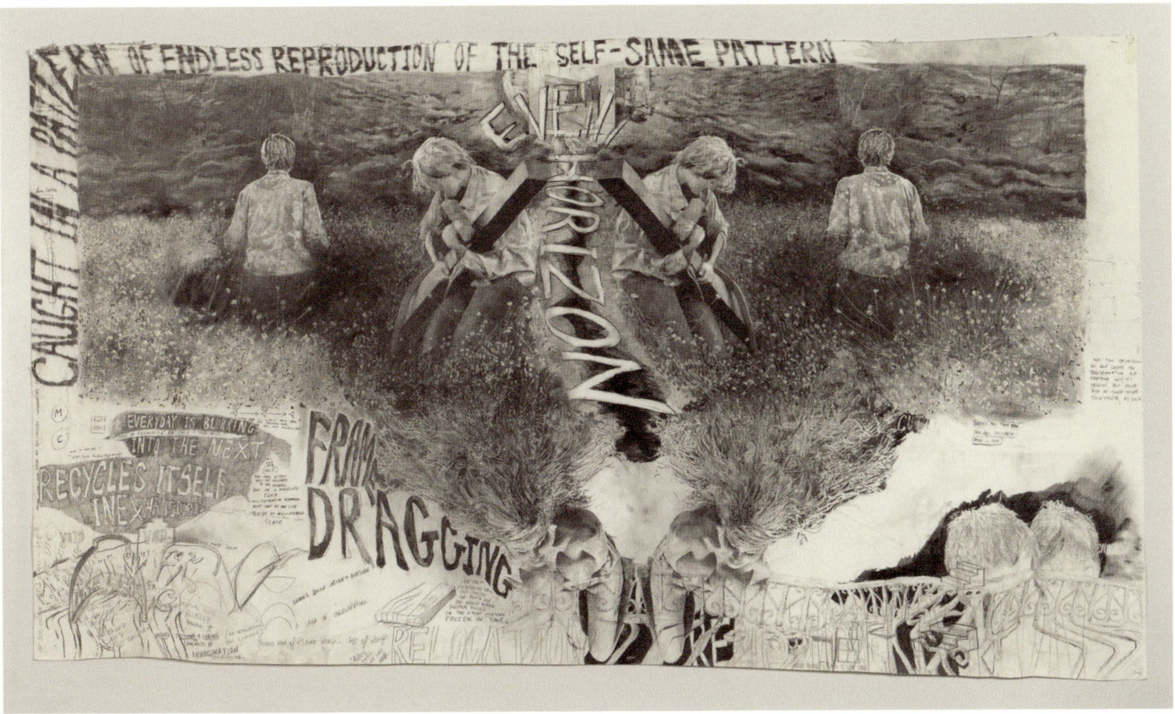
CAUGHT IN A PATTERN OF ENDLESS REPRODUCTION OF THE SELF-SAME PATTERN
HORIZON
EVERYDAY IS BLURRING
INTO THE NEXT
RECYCLES ITSELF
FROM
DRAGGING

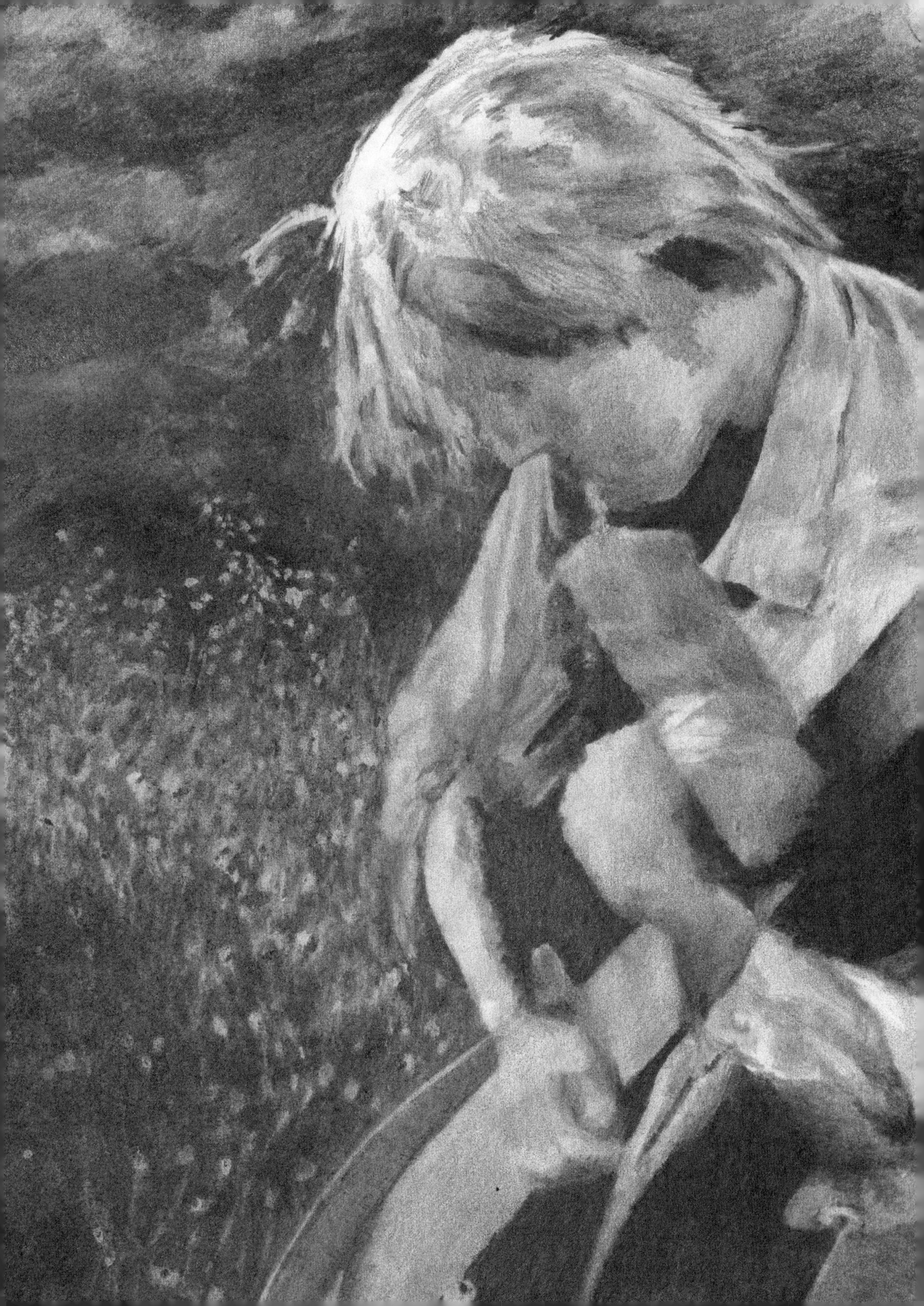

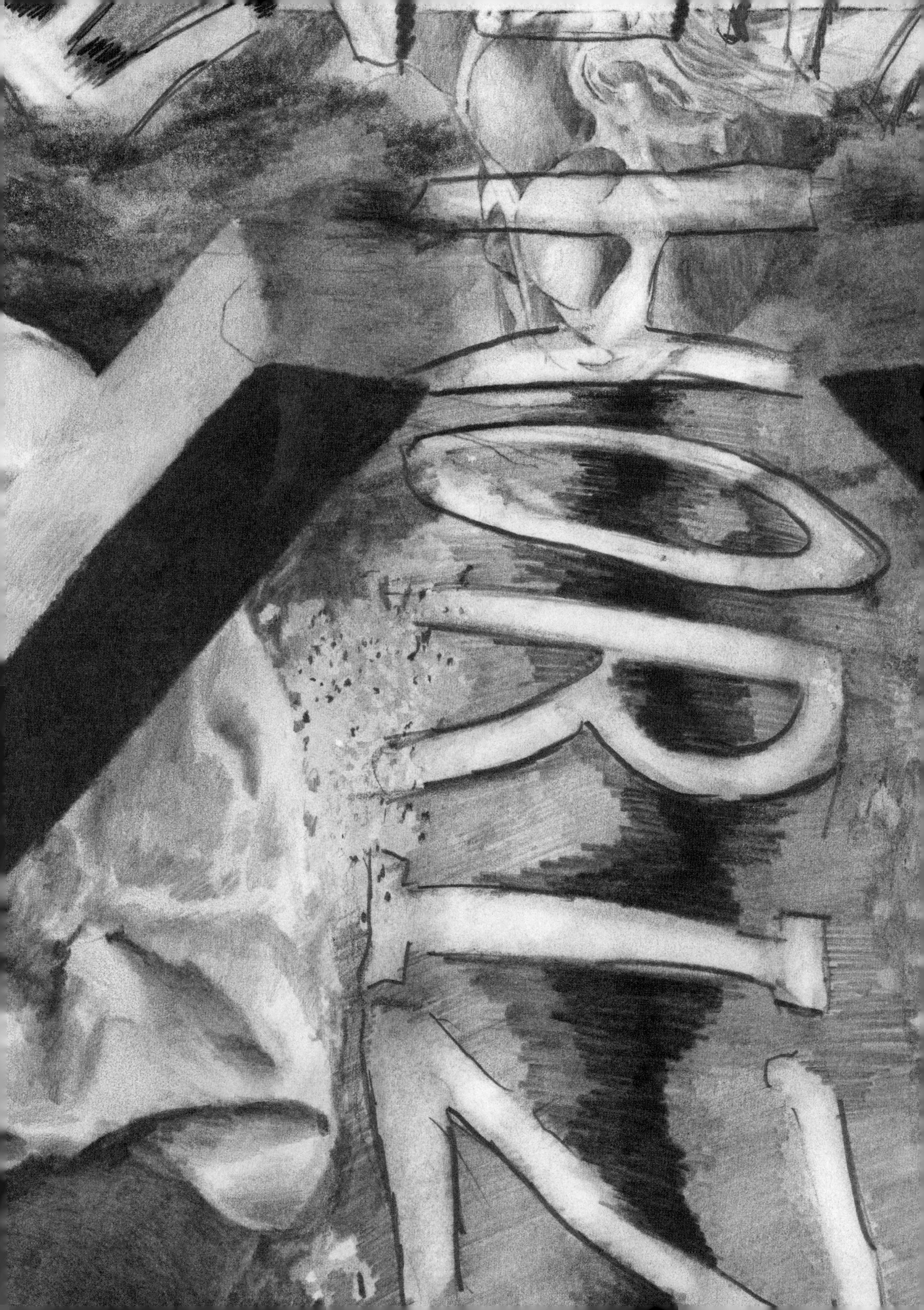

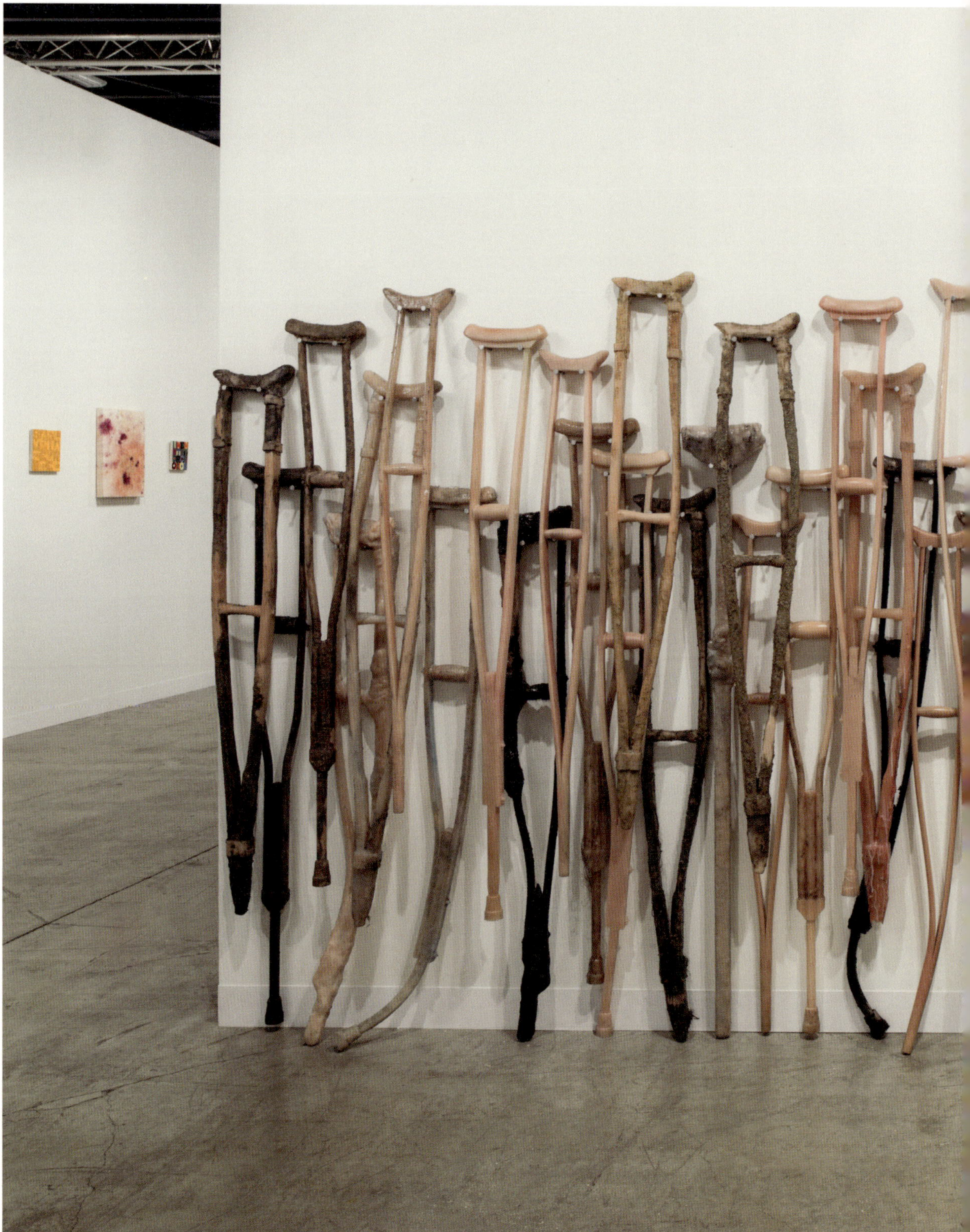

Cult of Invalidism, 2012

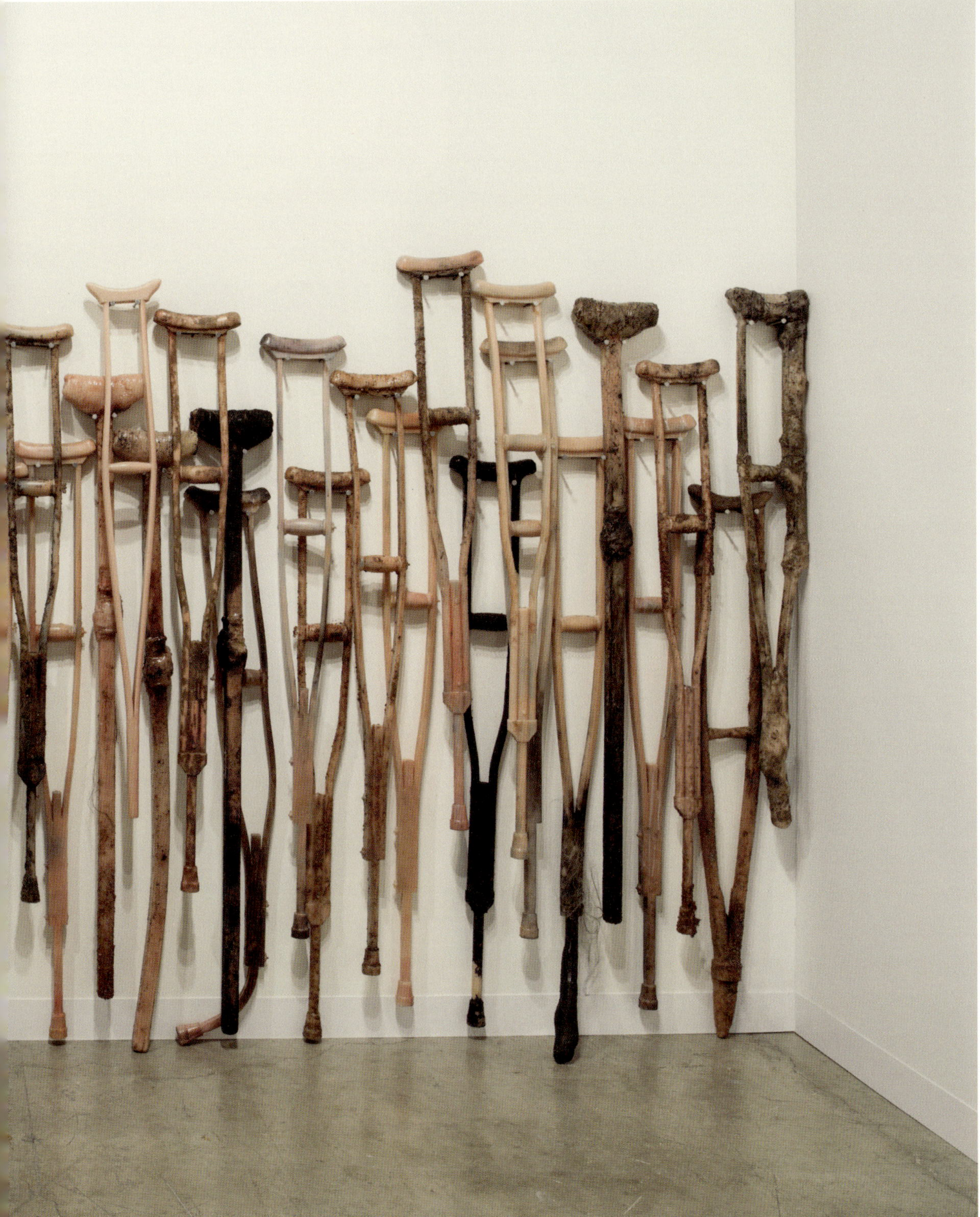

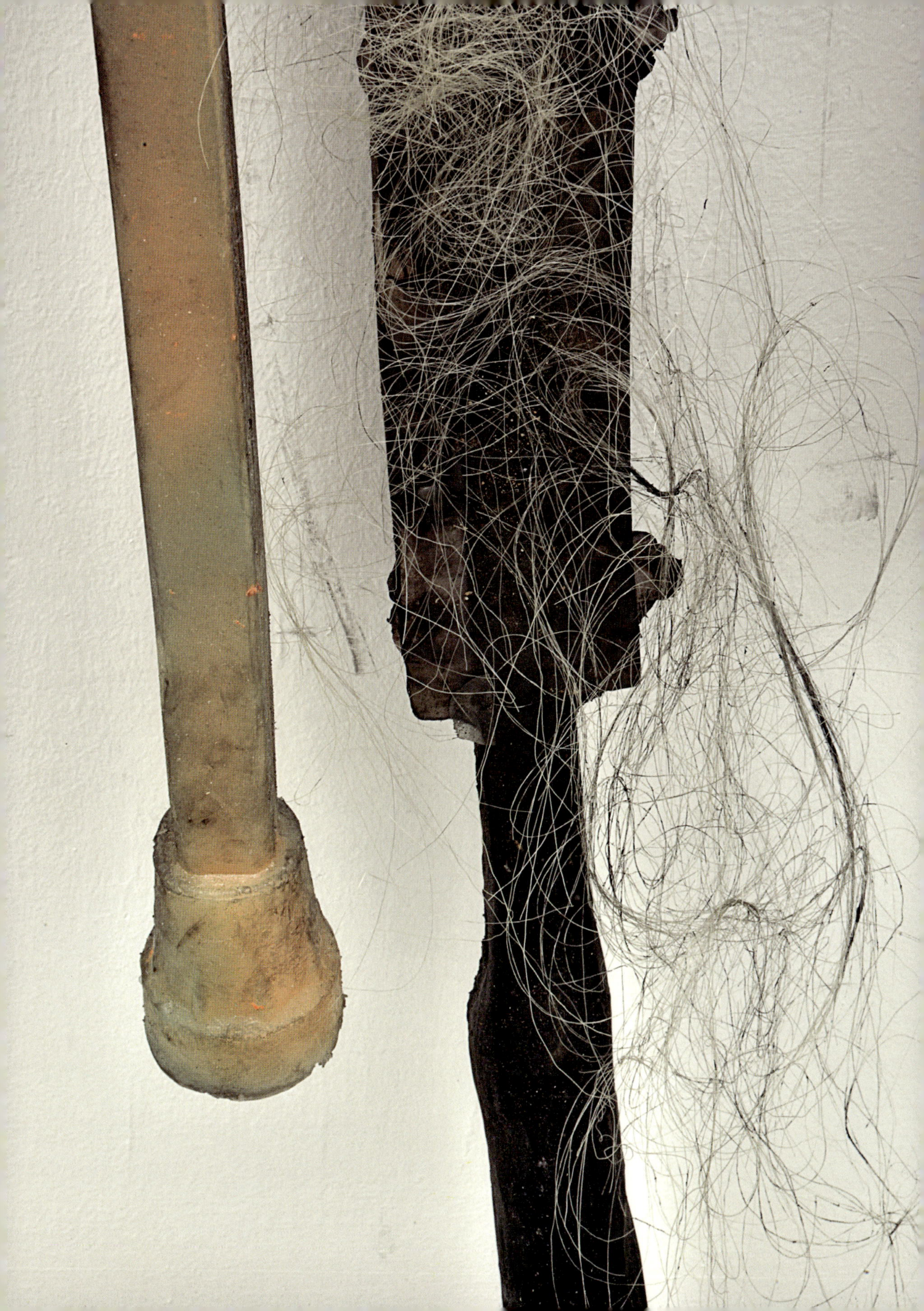

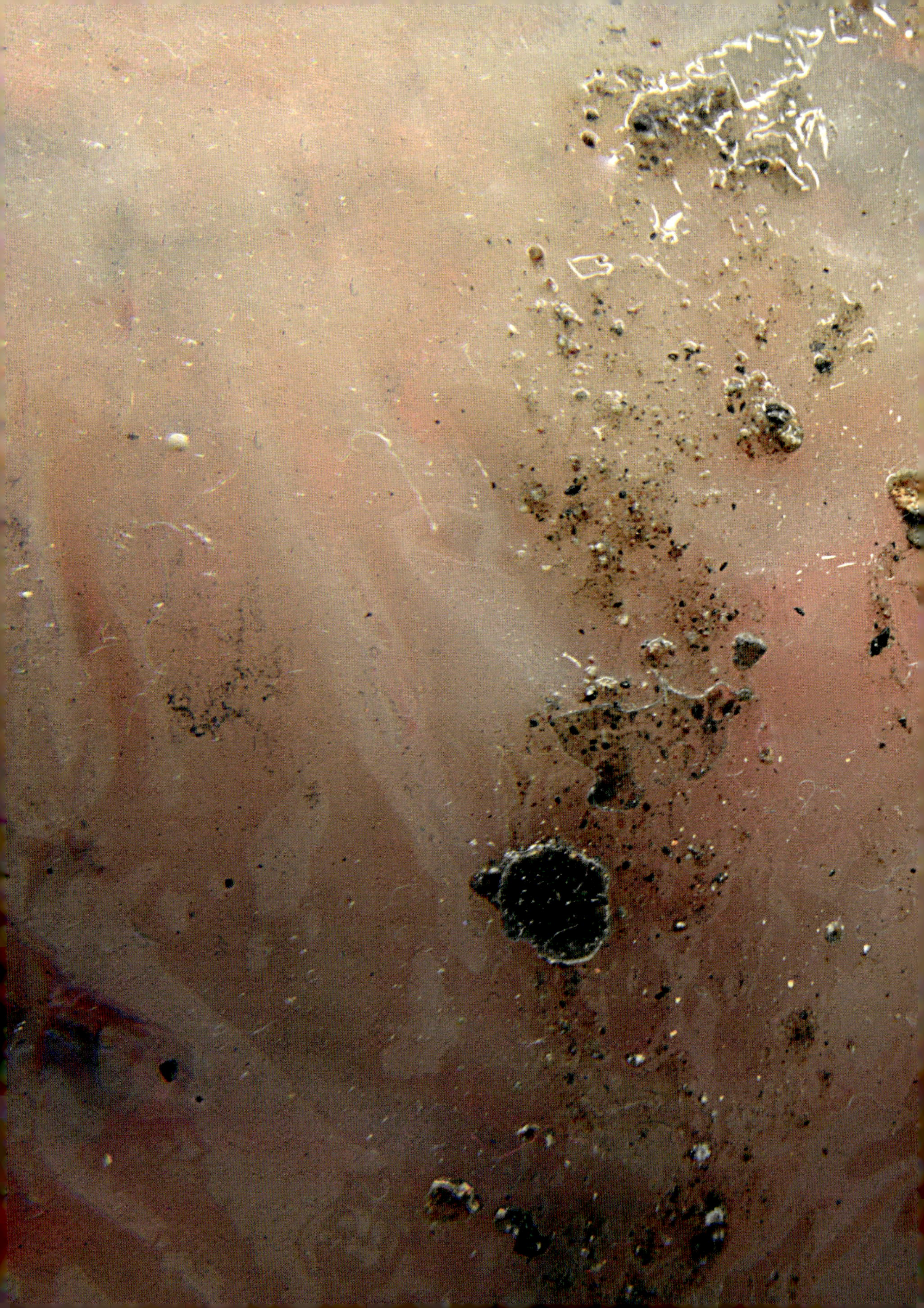

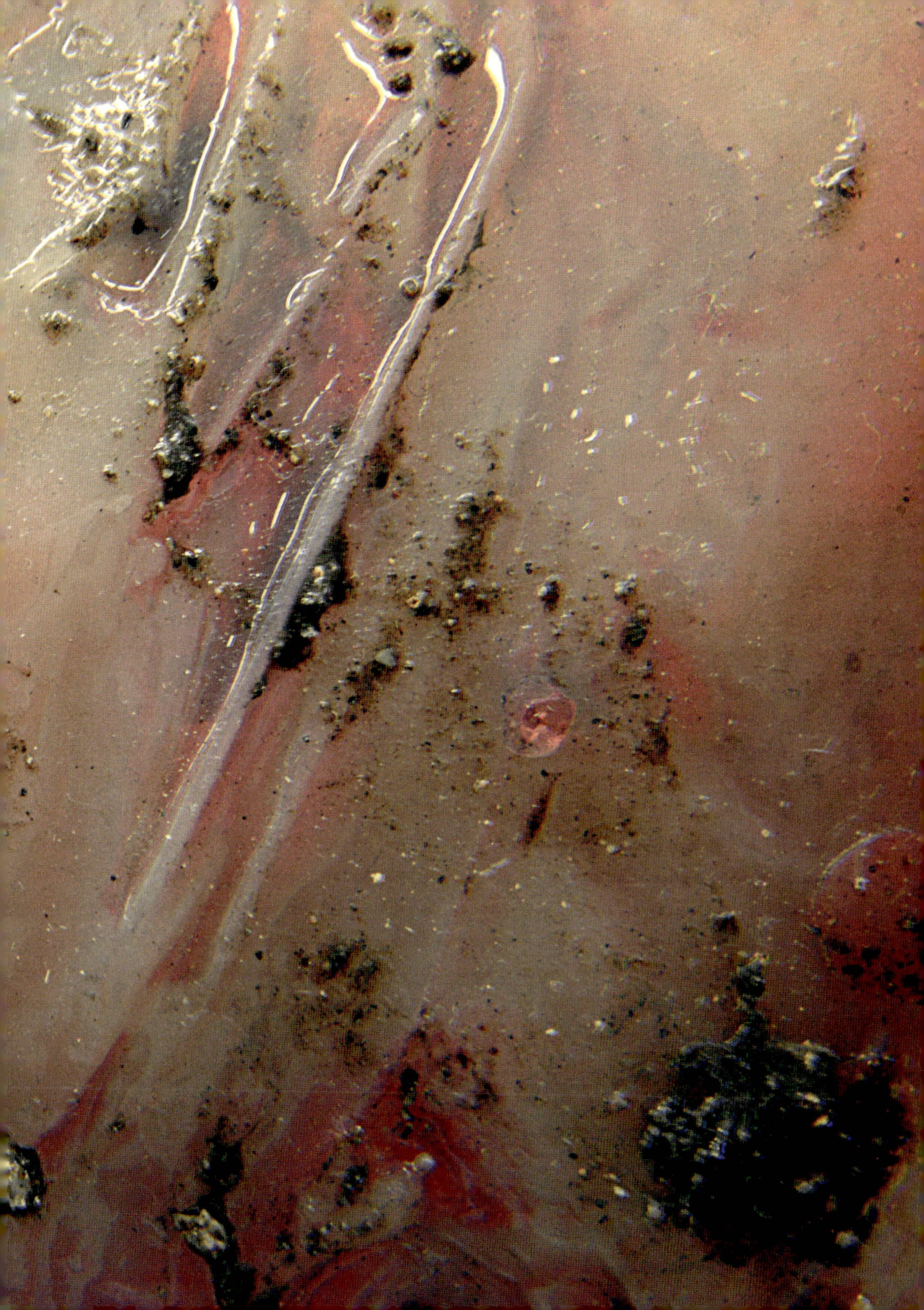

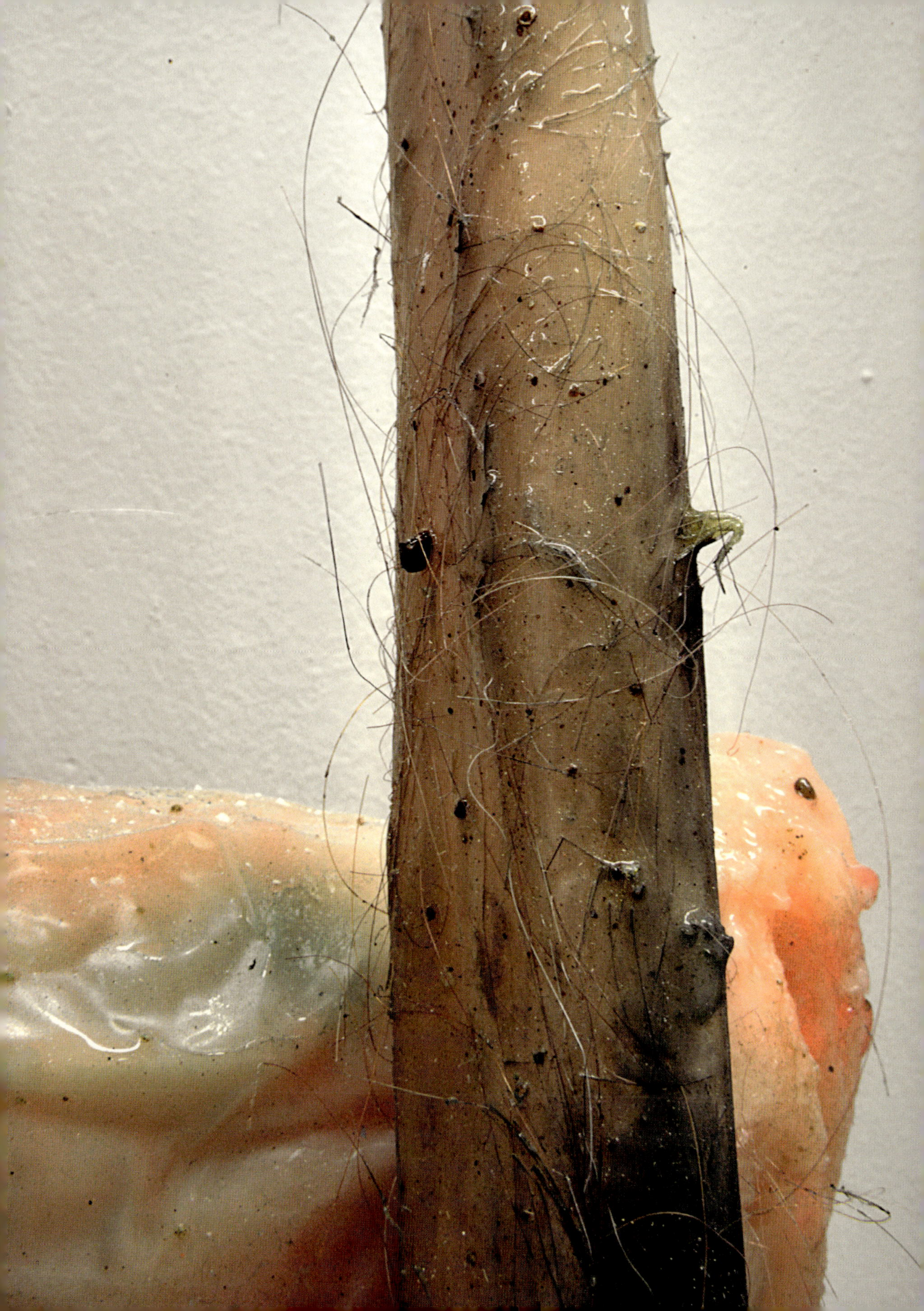

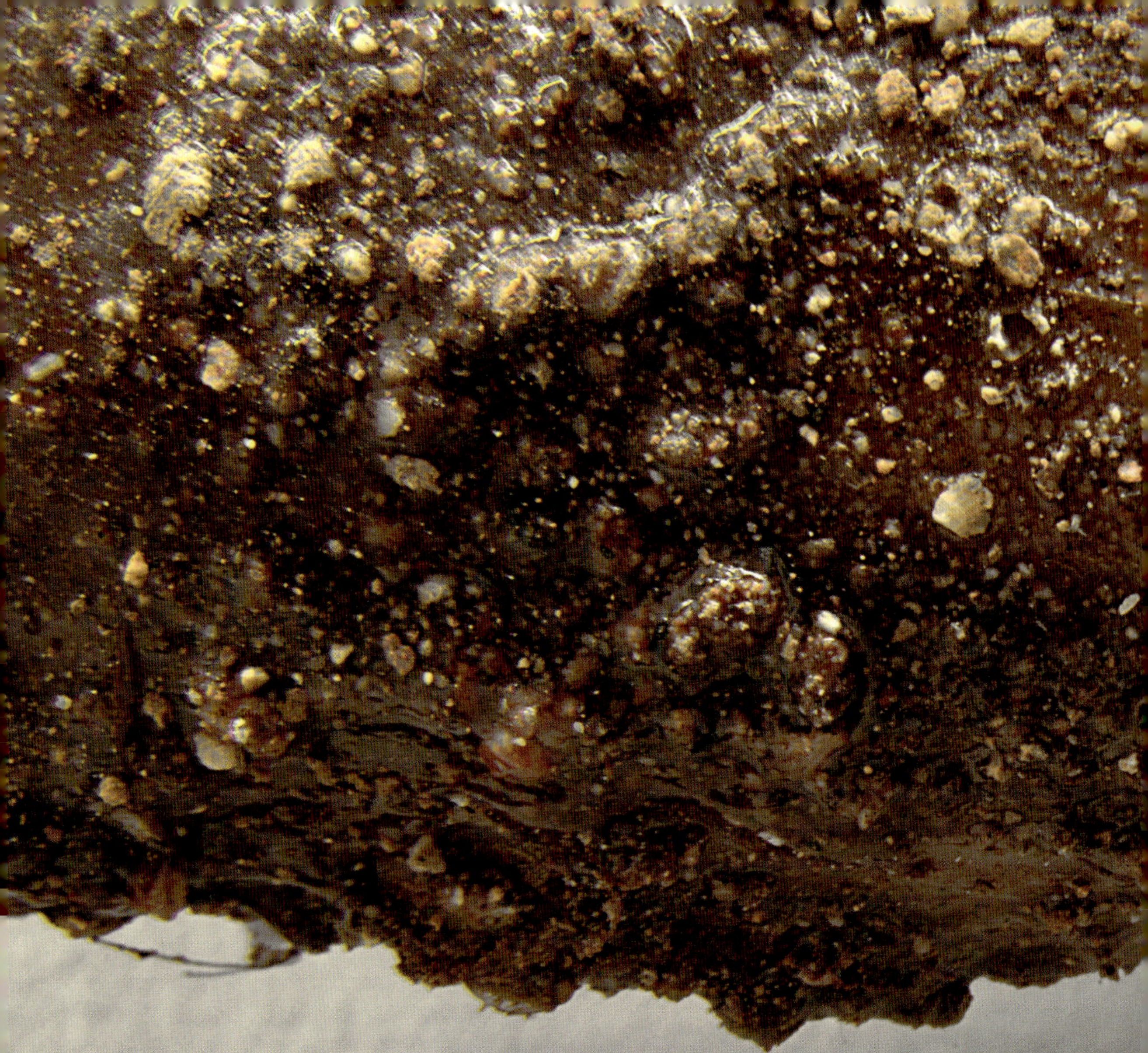

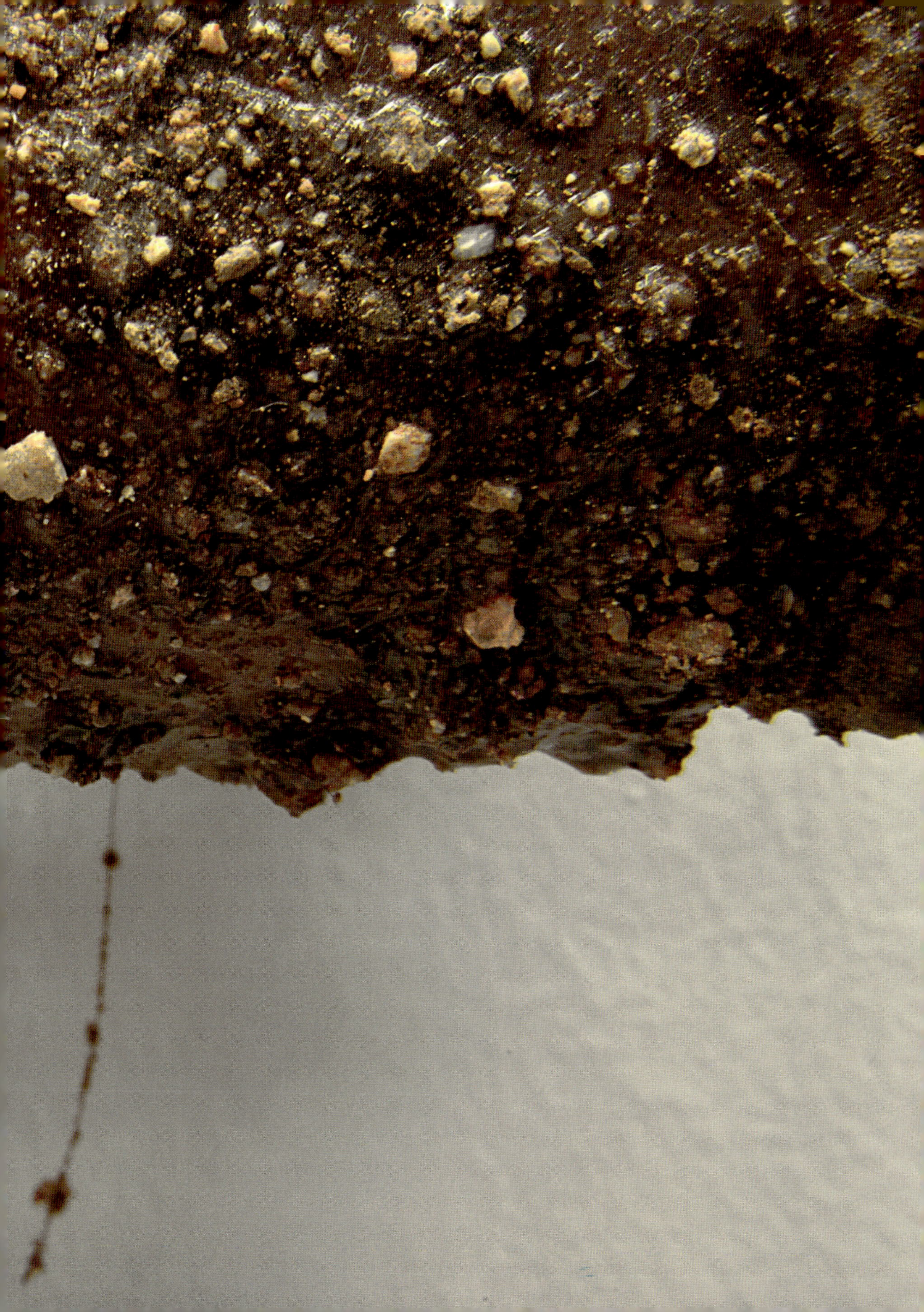

End Is Where We Start From, 2013

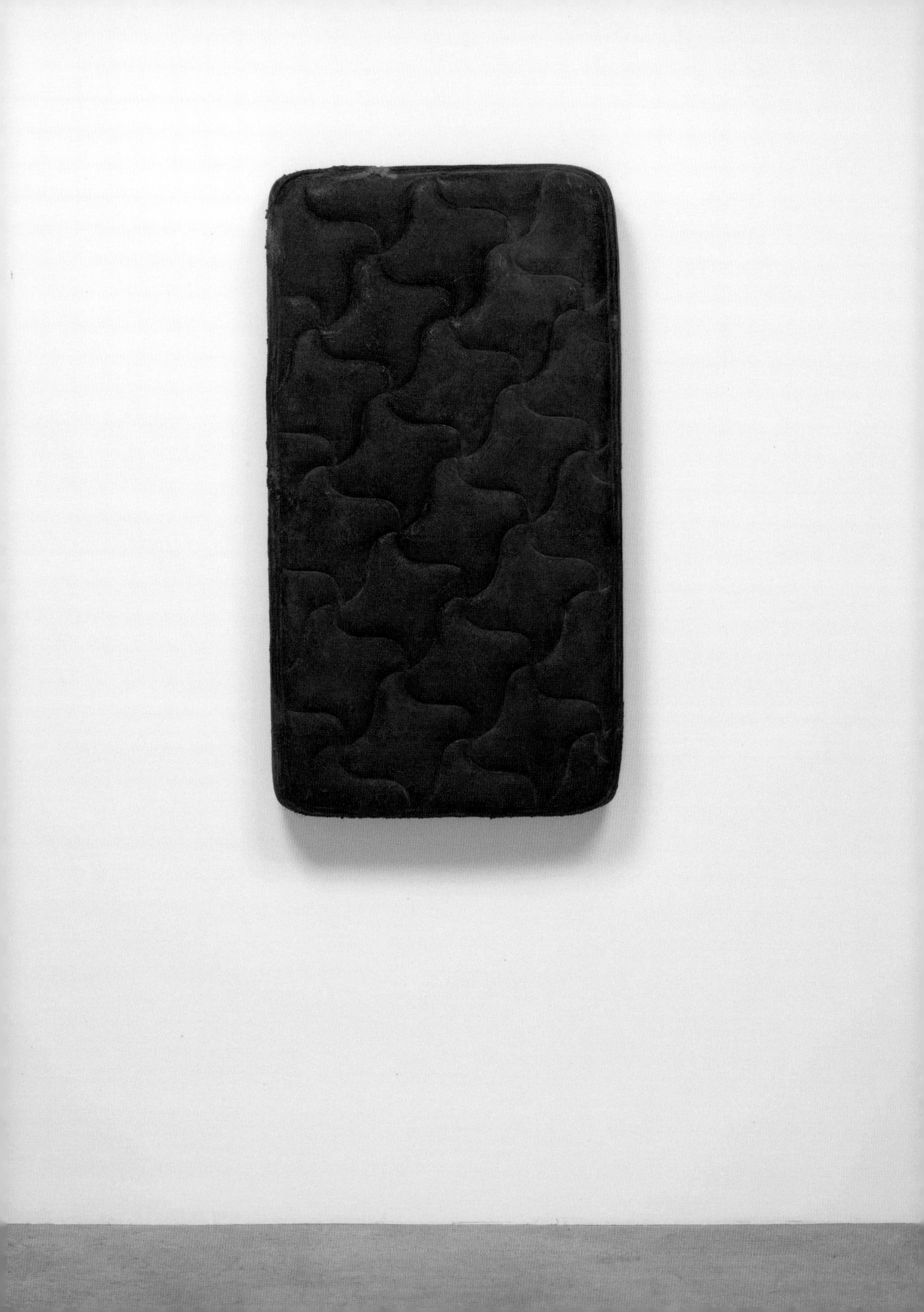

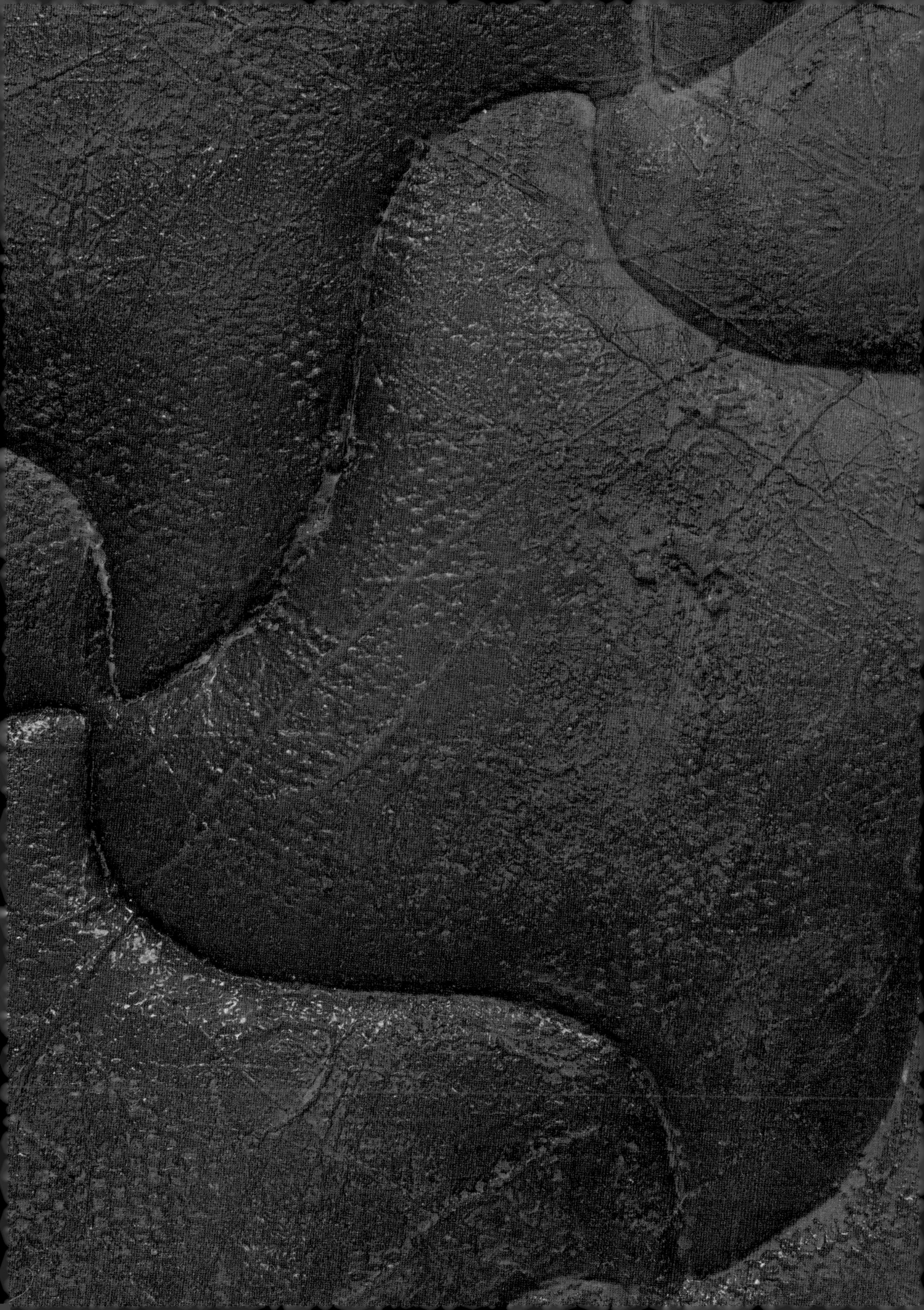

226, 2013

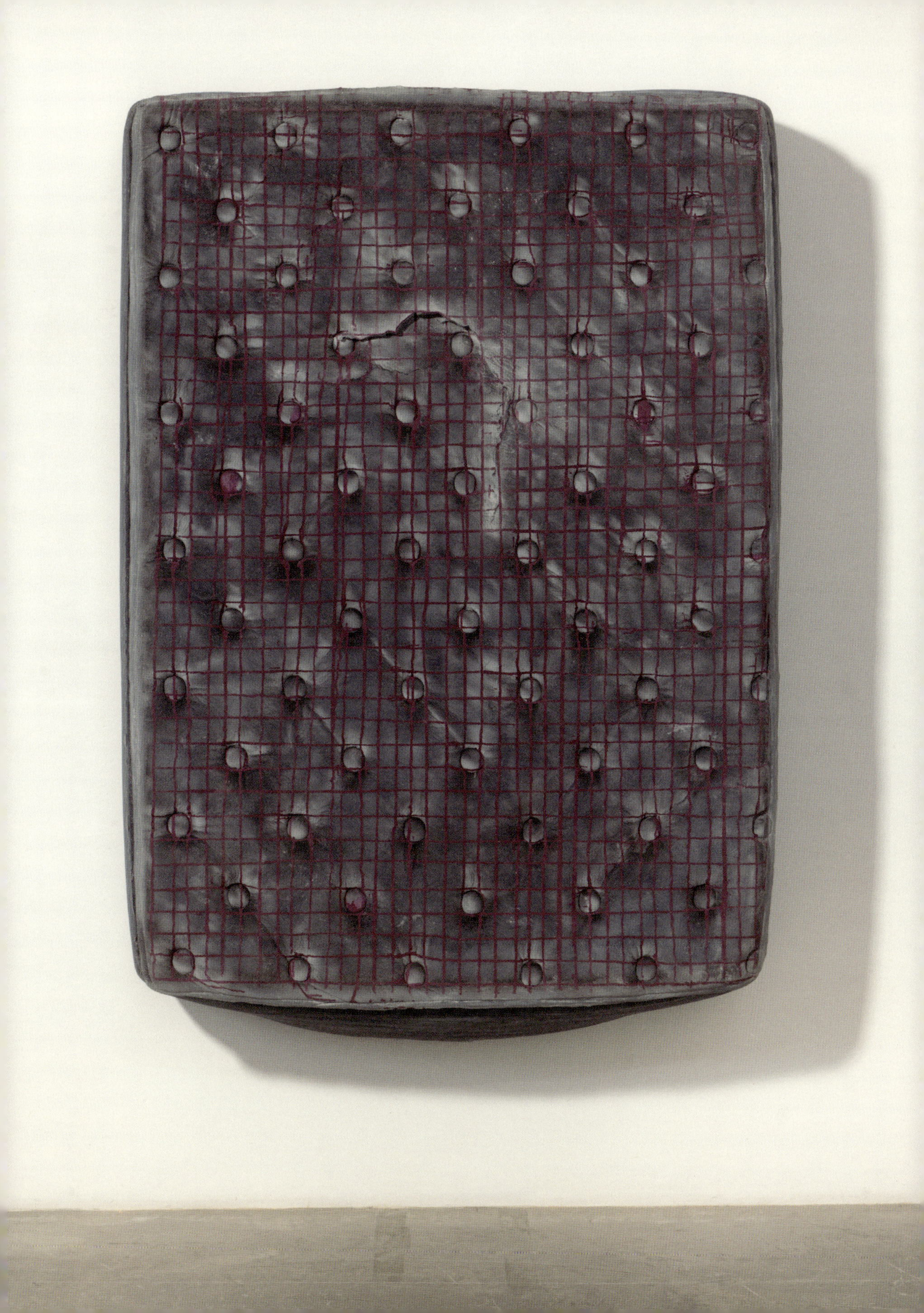

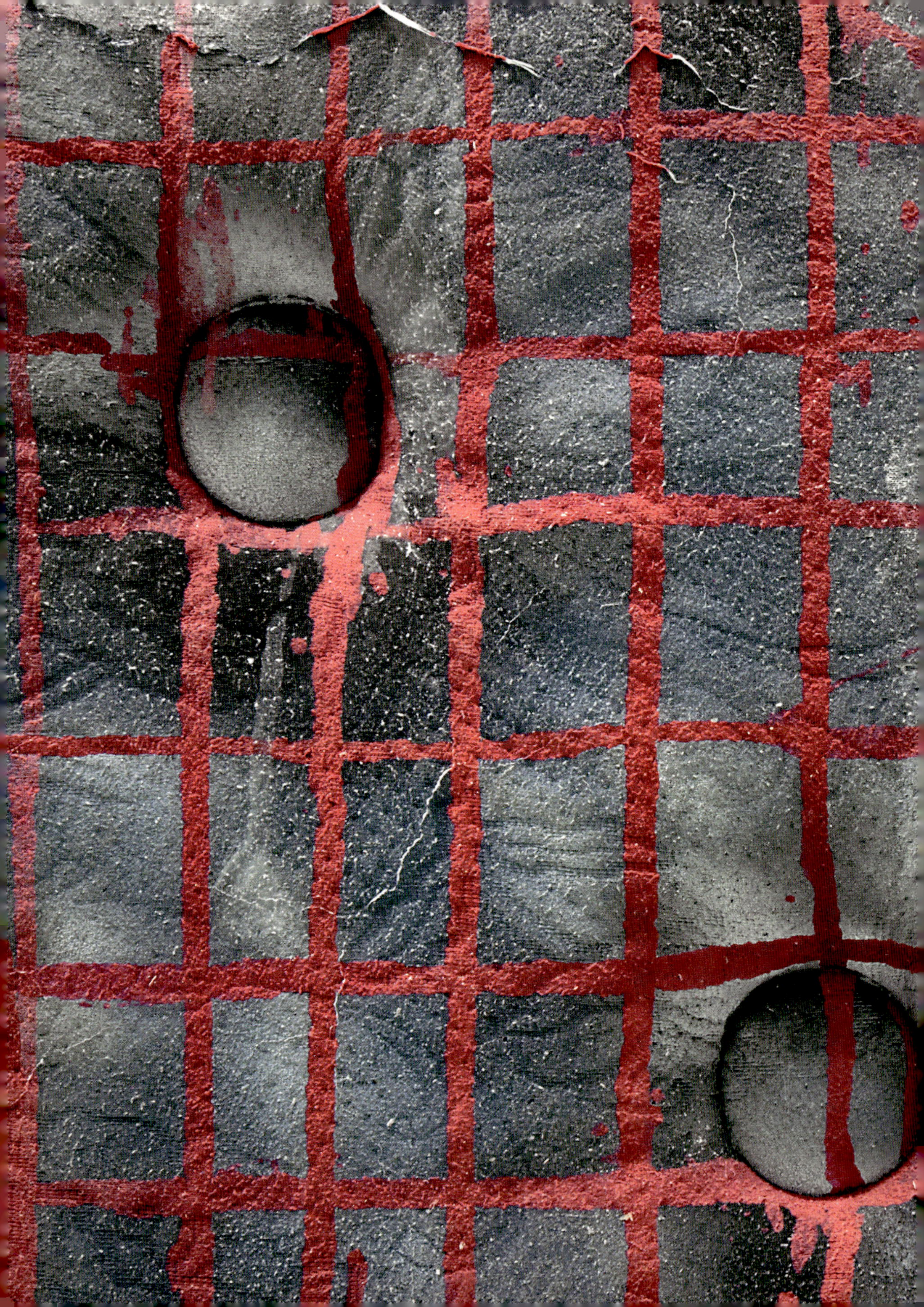

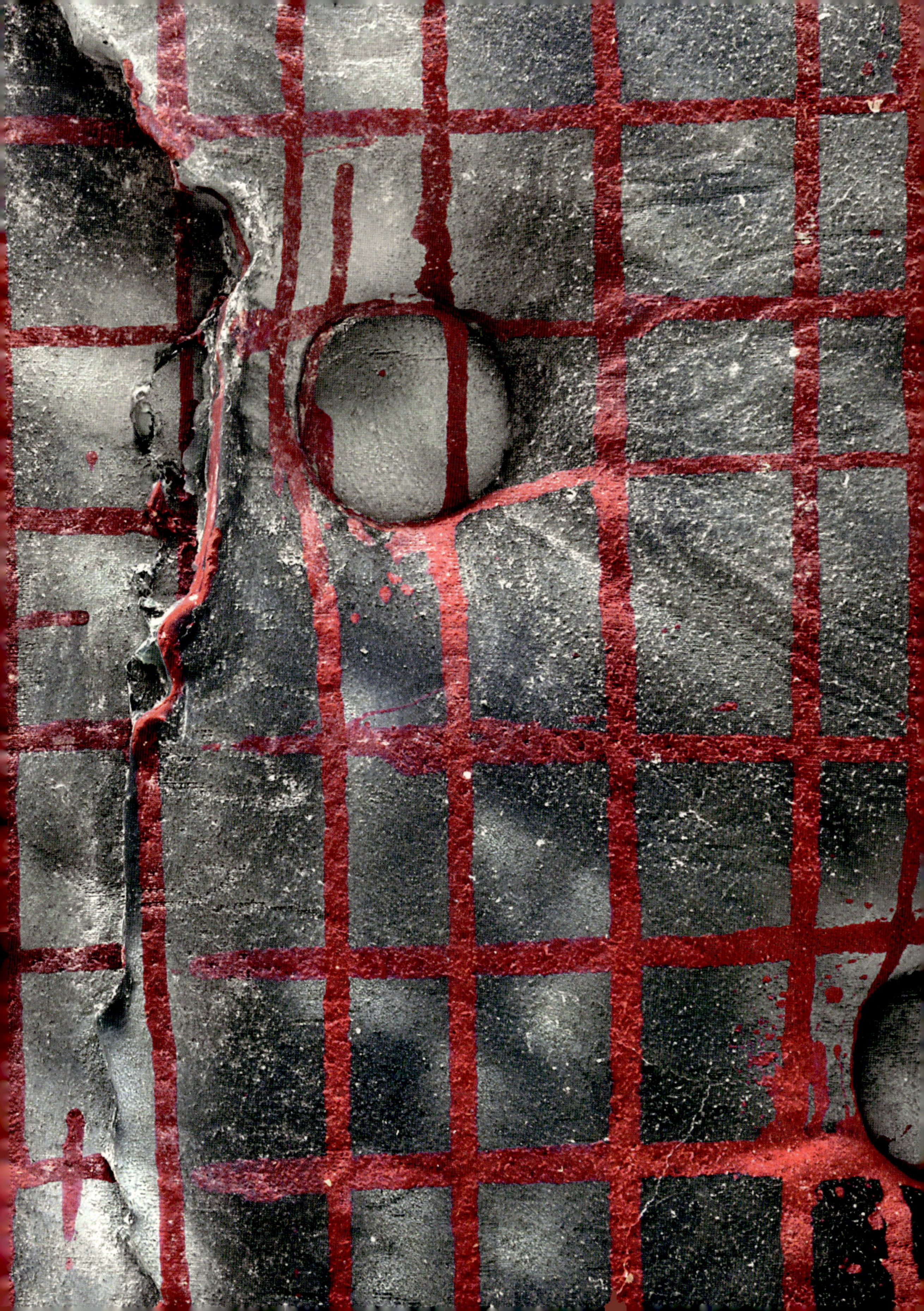

192, 2013

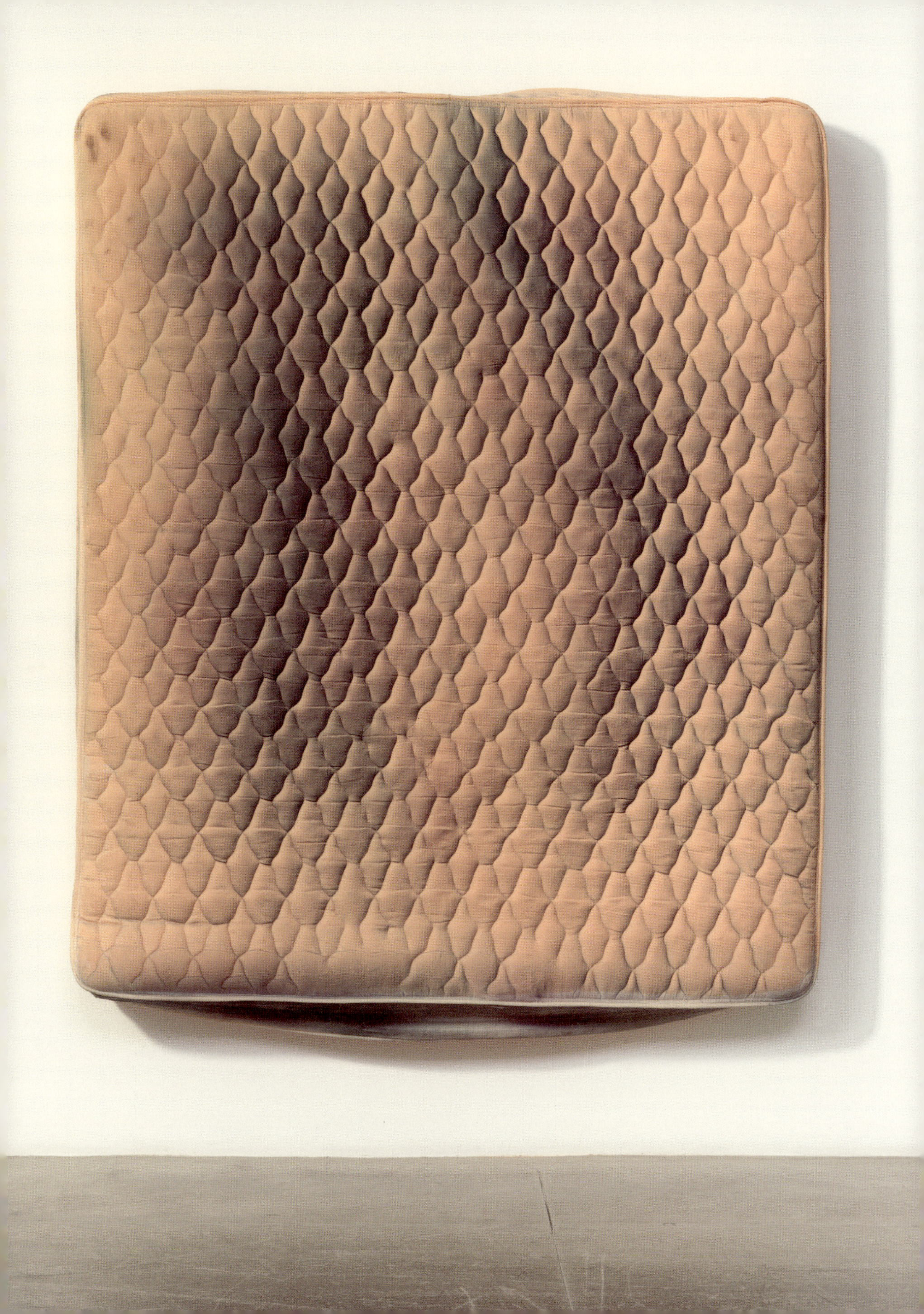

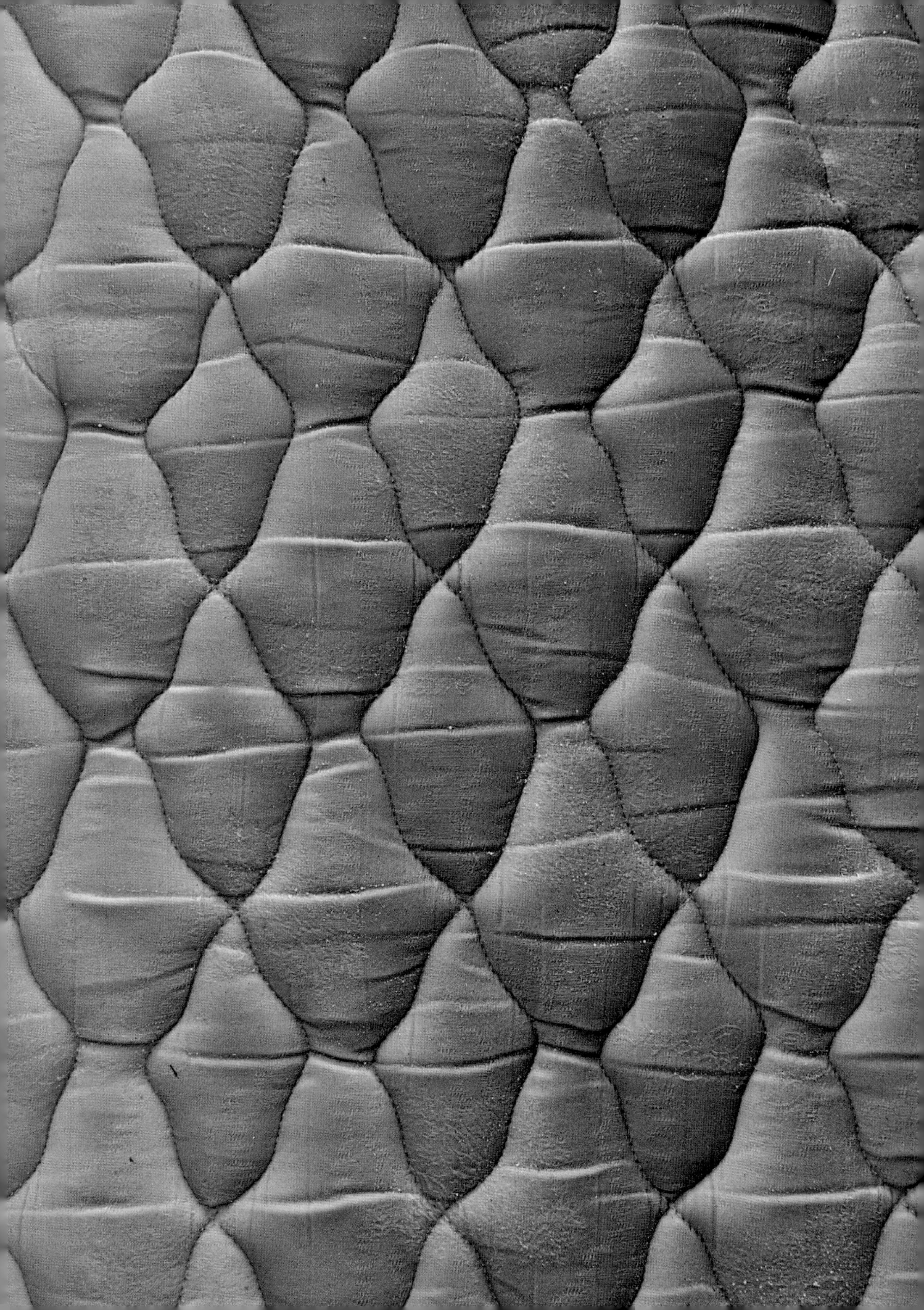

Who's Afraid of Red, Yellow, and Blue, 2014

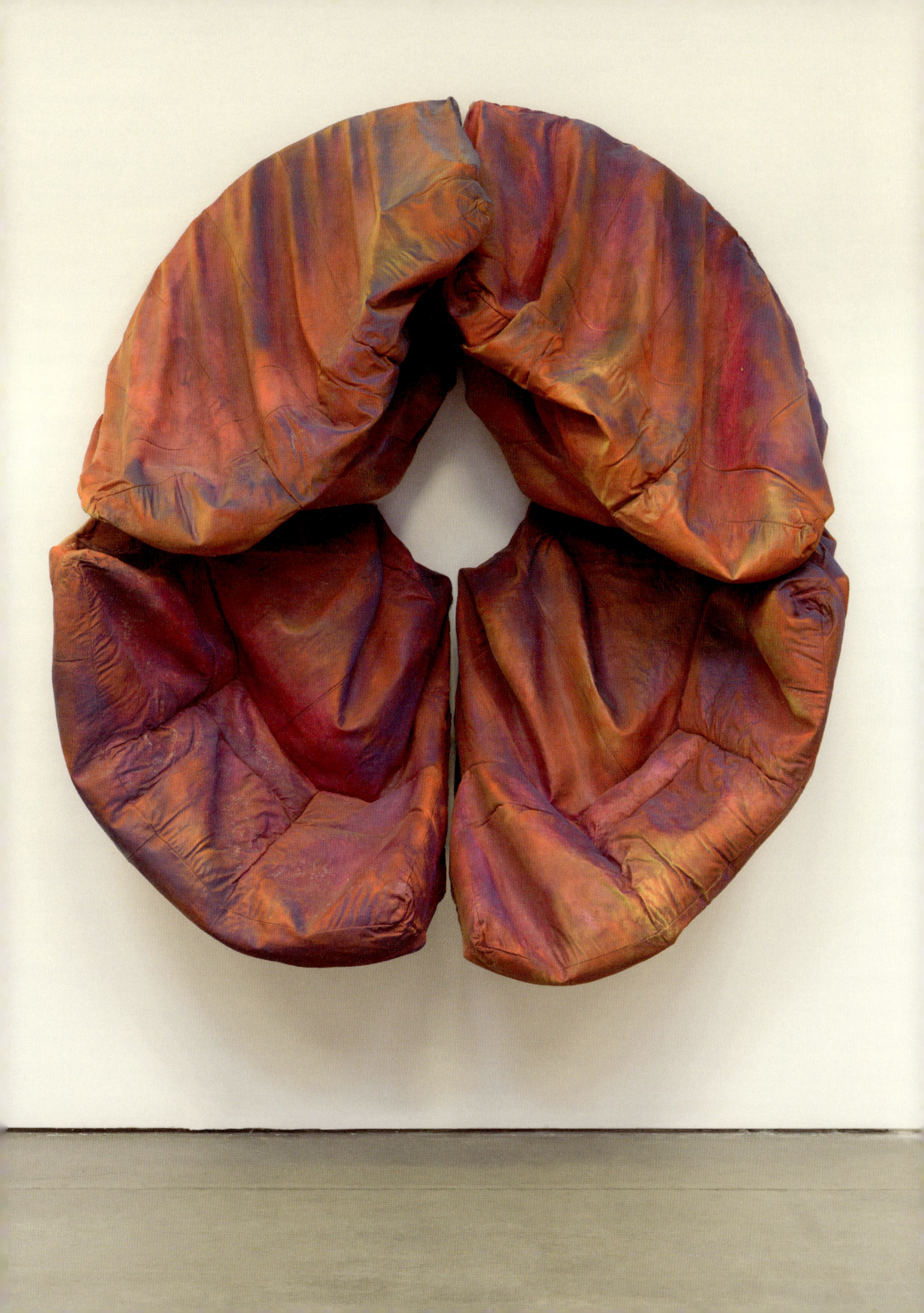

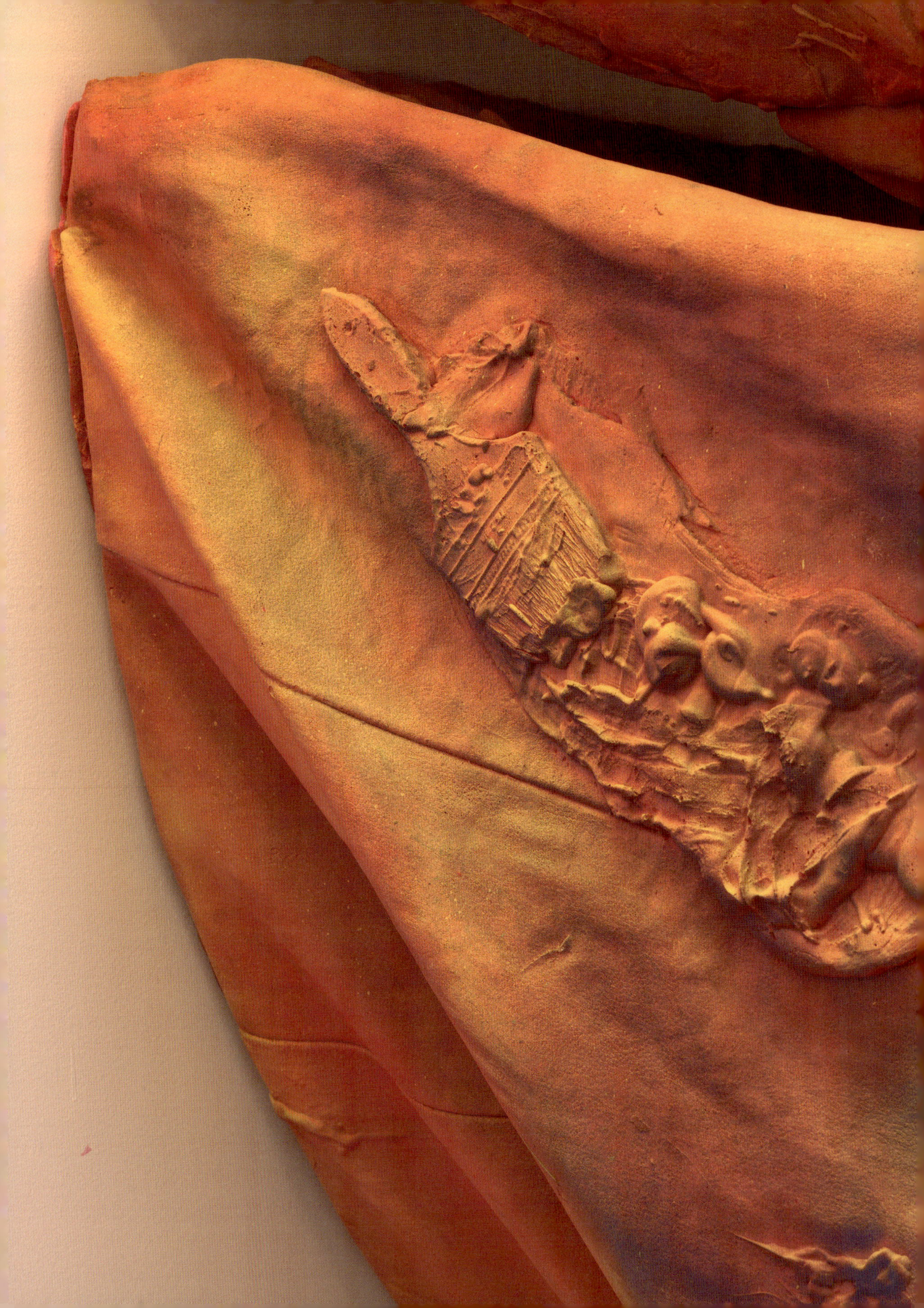

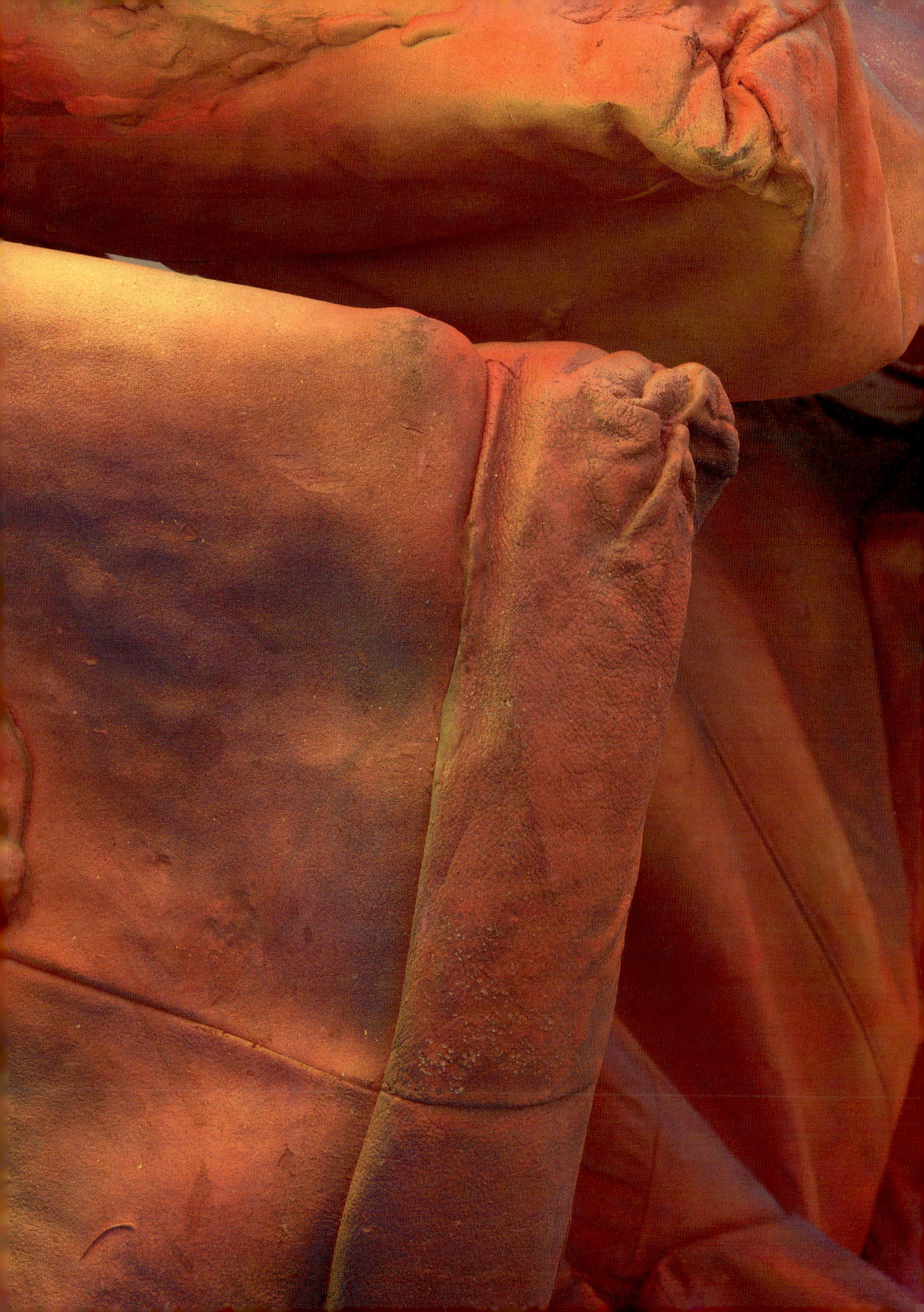

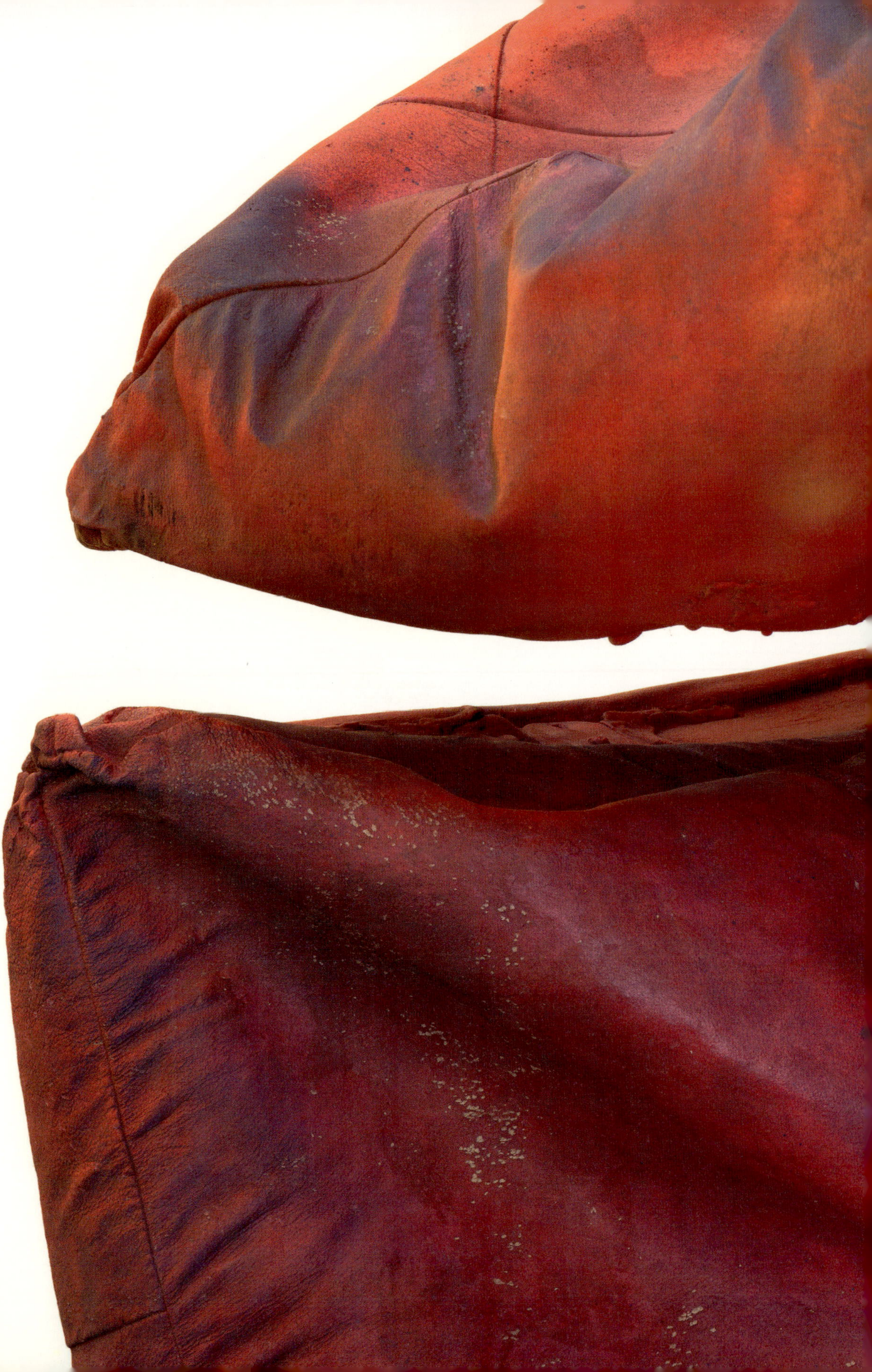

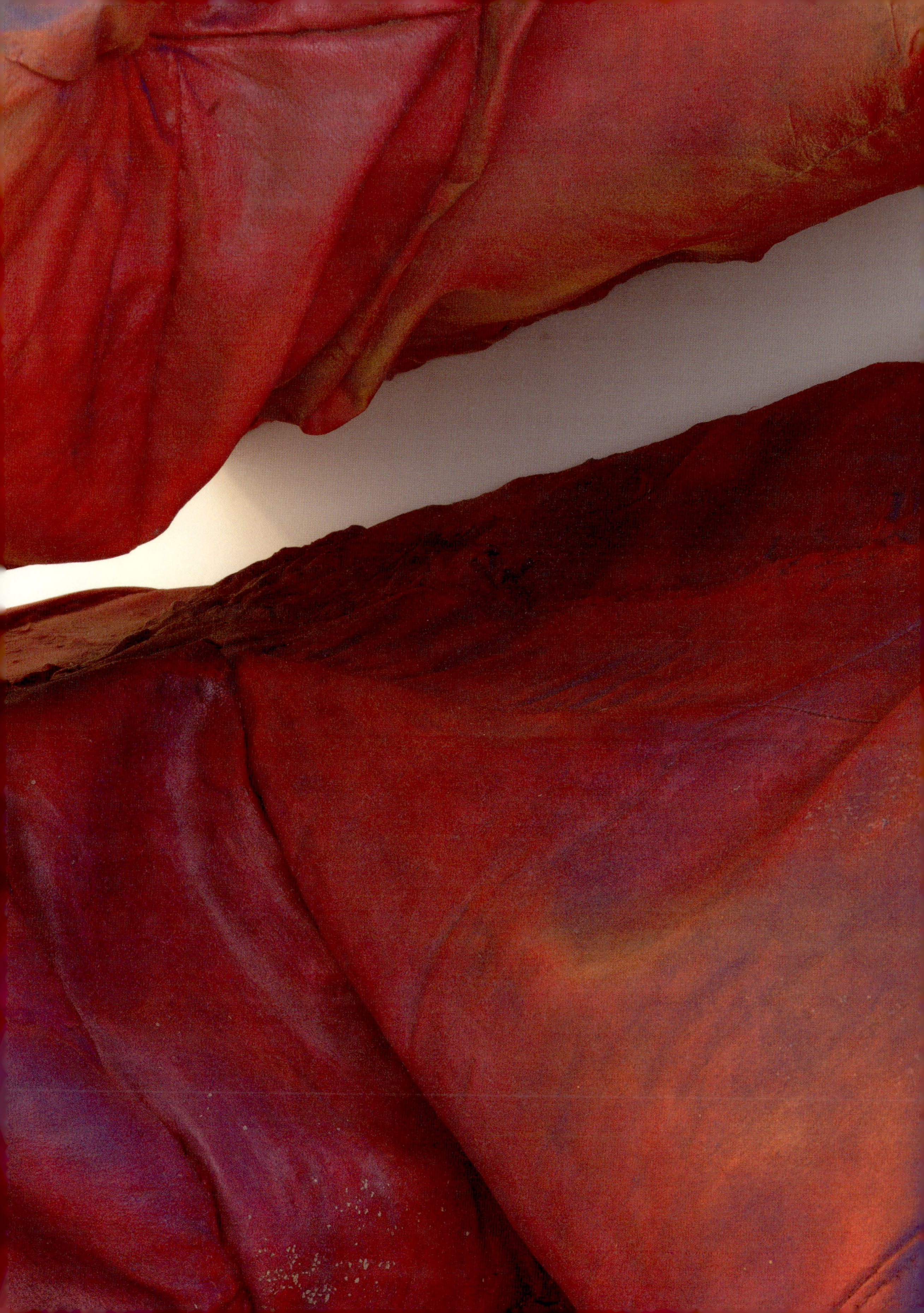

Door (closet), 2014–2016

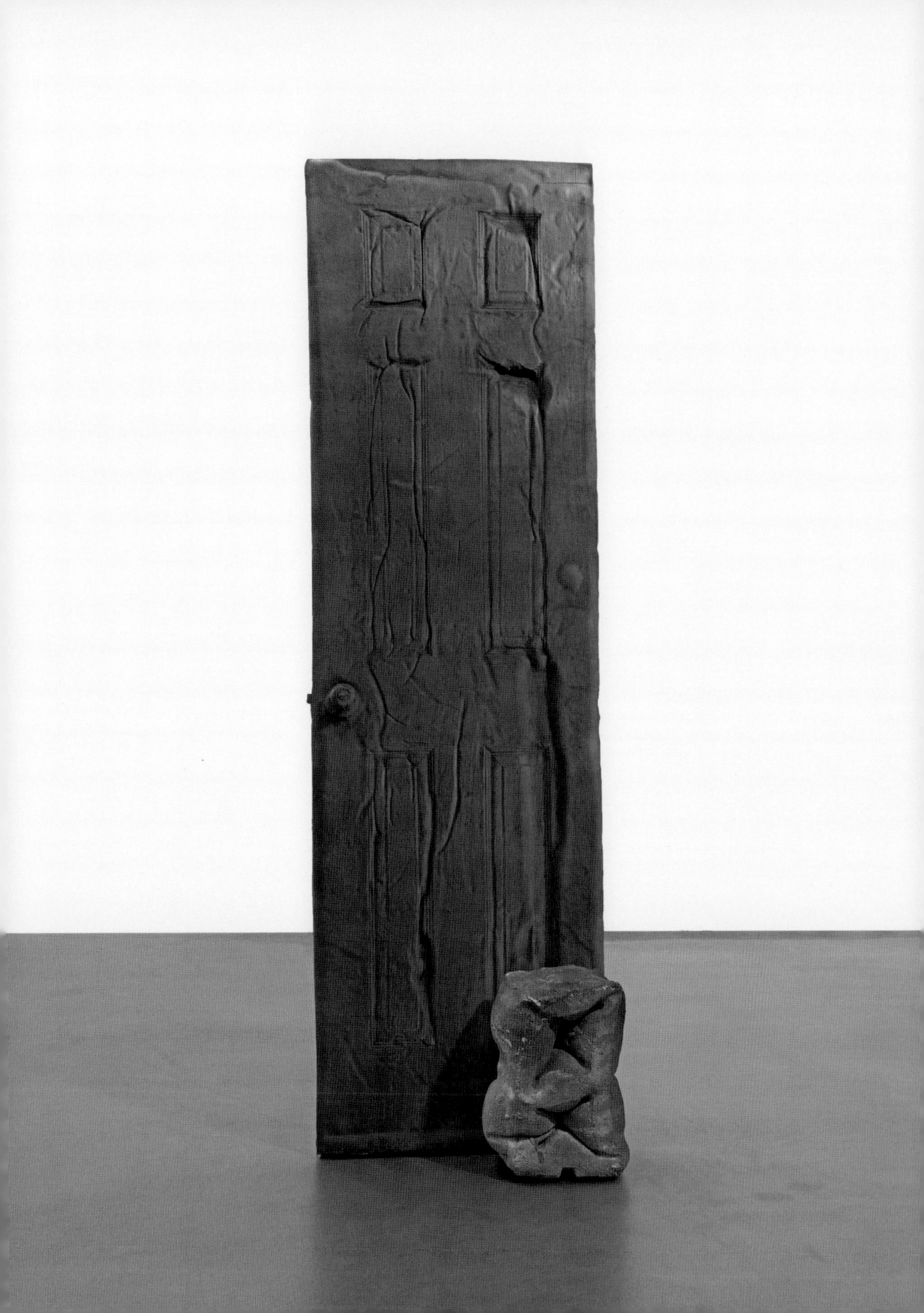

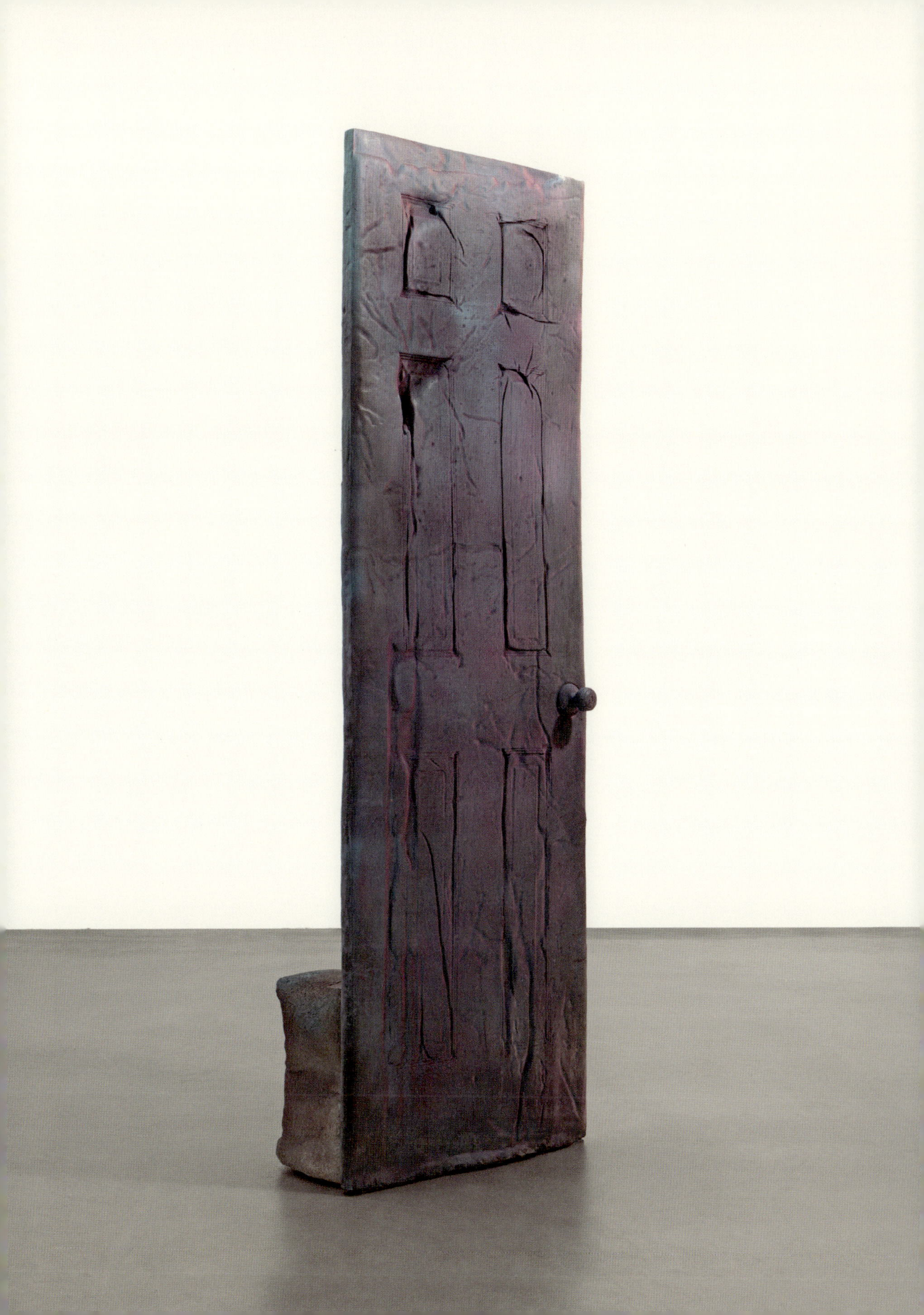

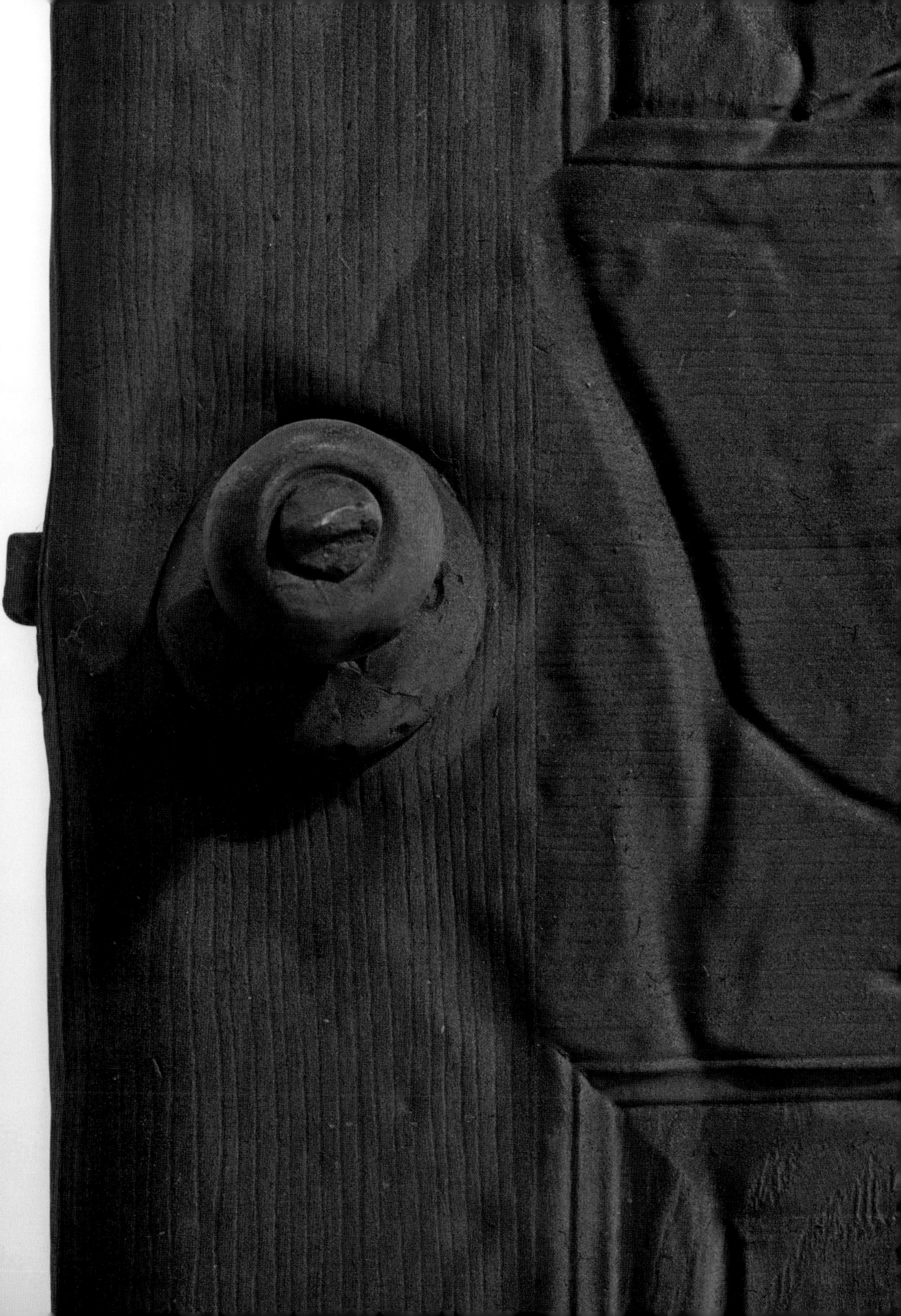

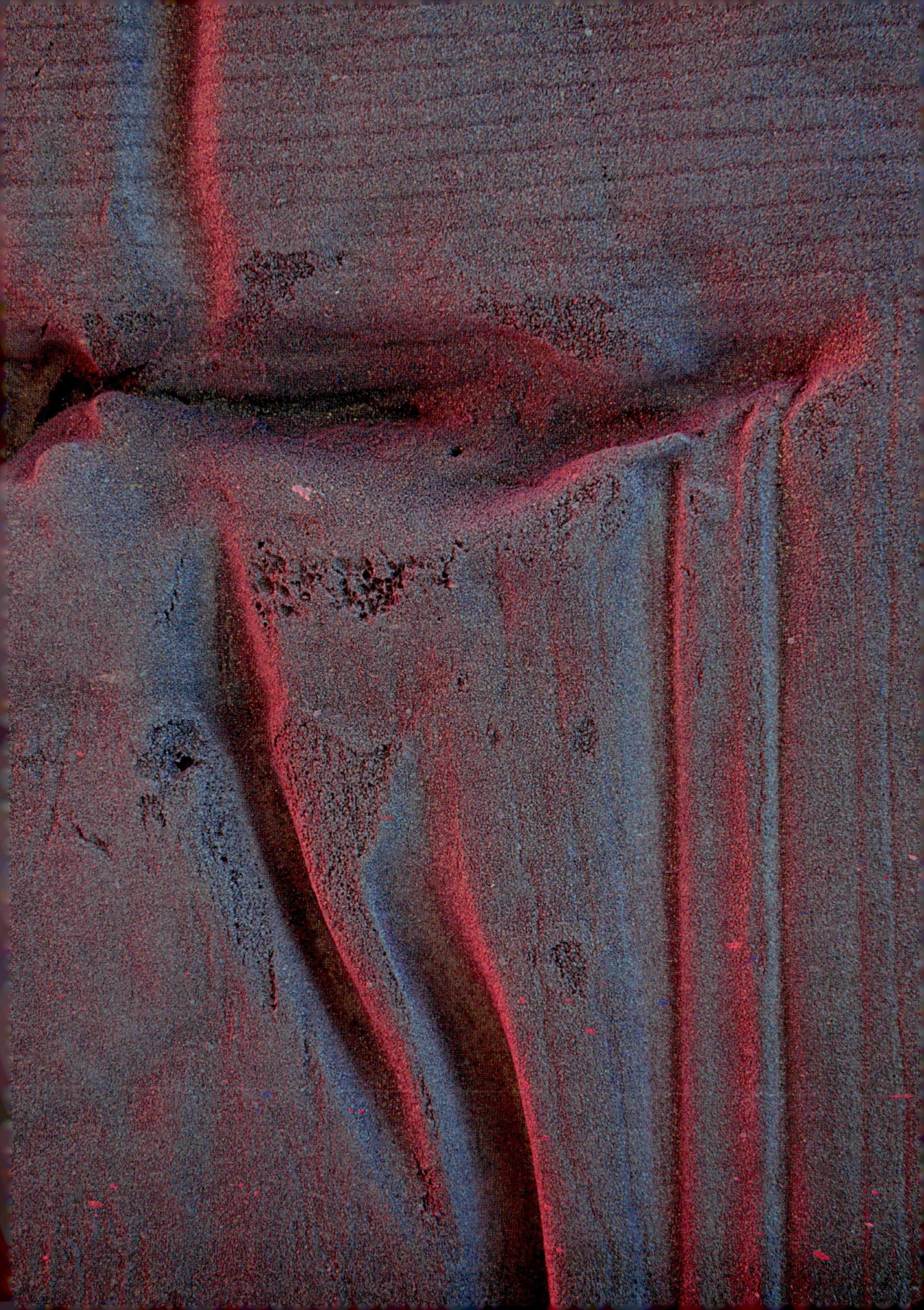

Position 4.8, 2015

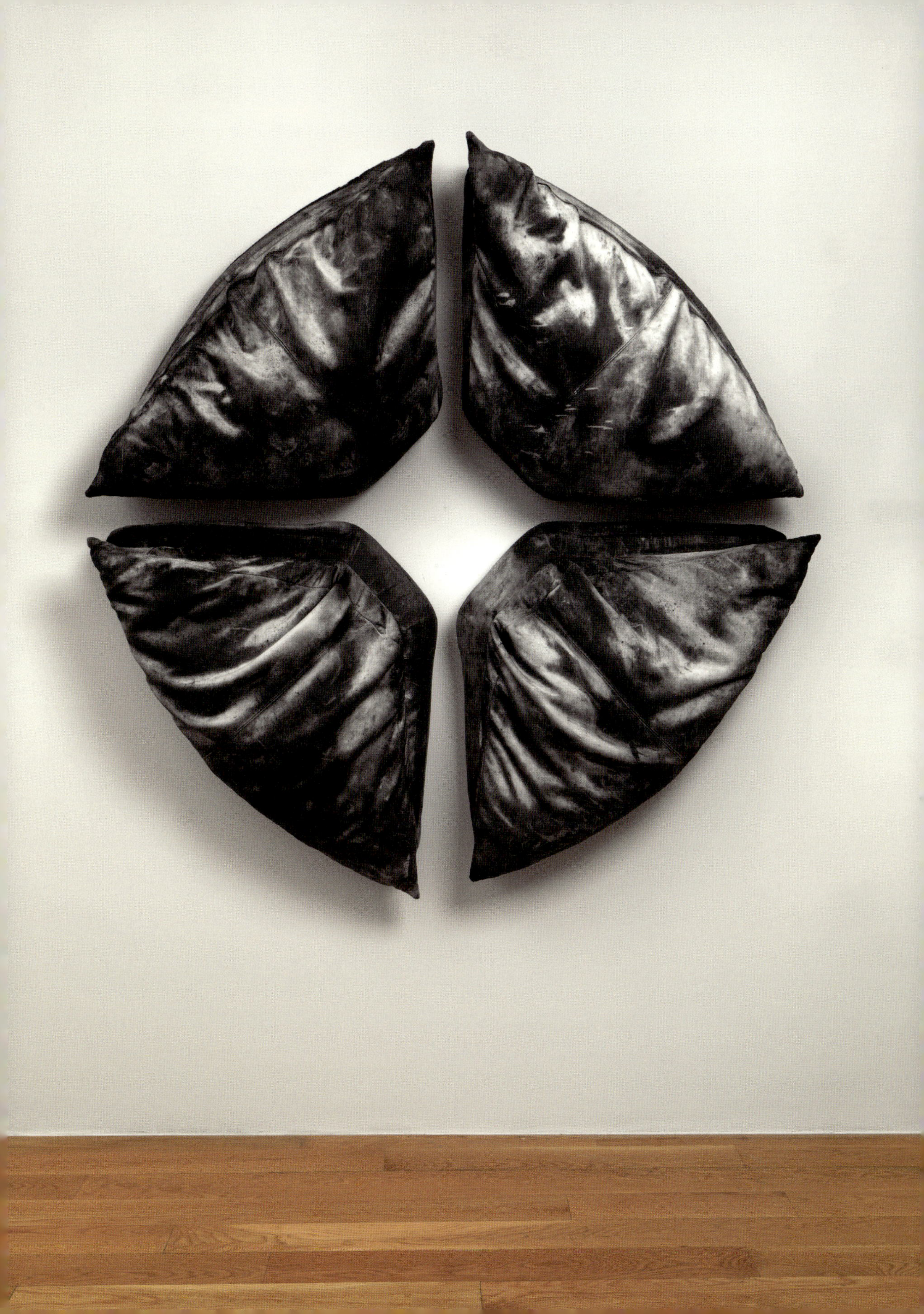

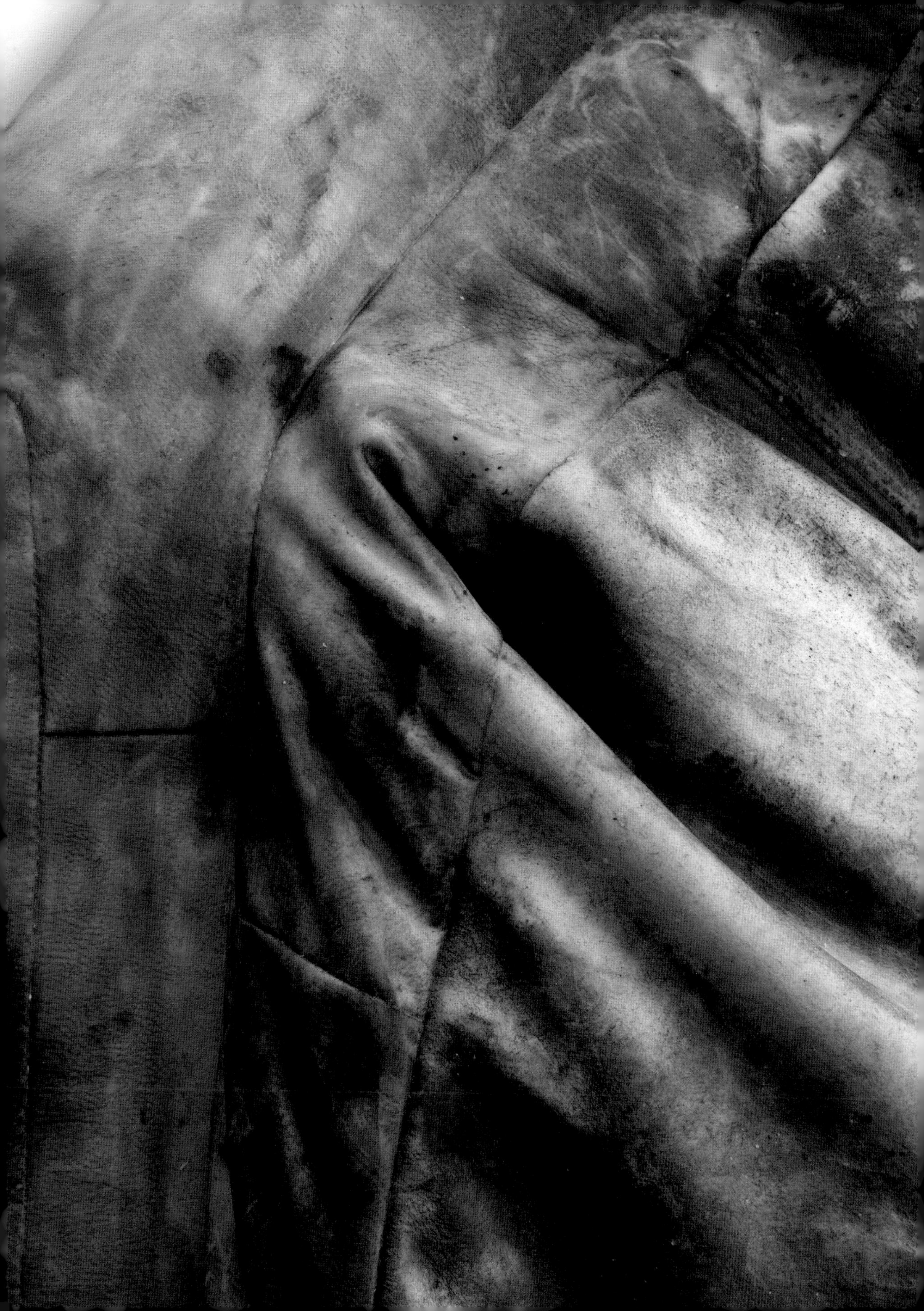

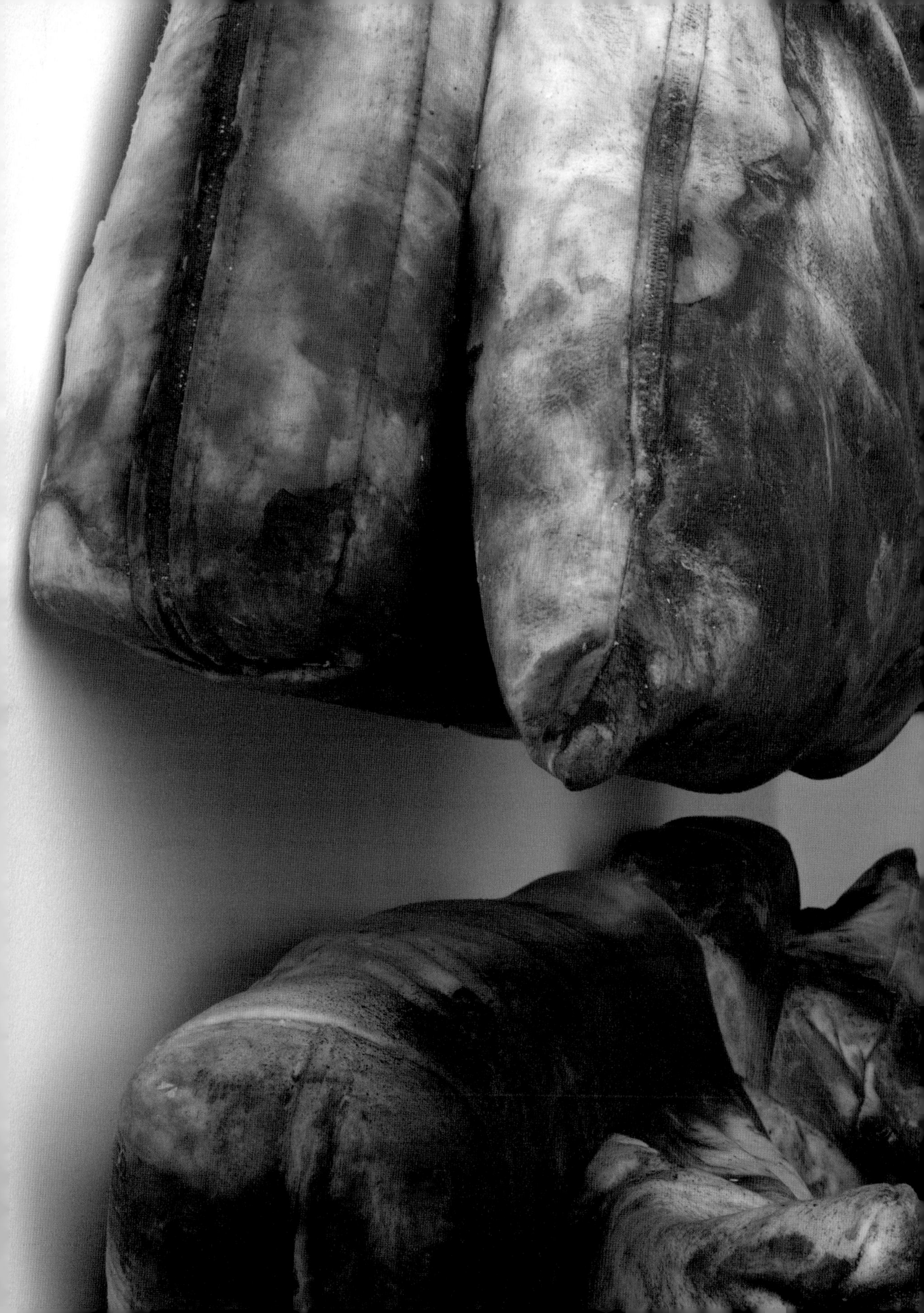

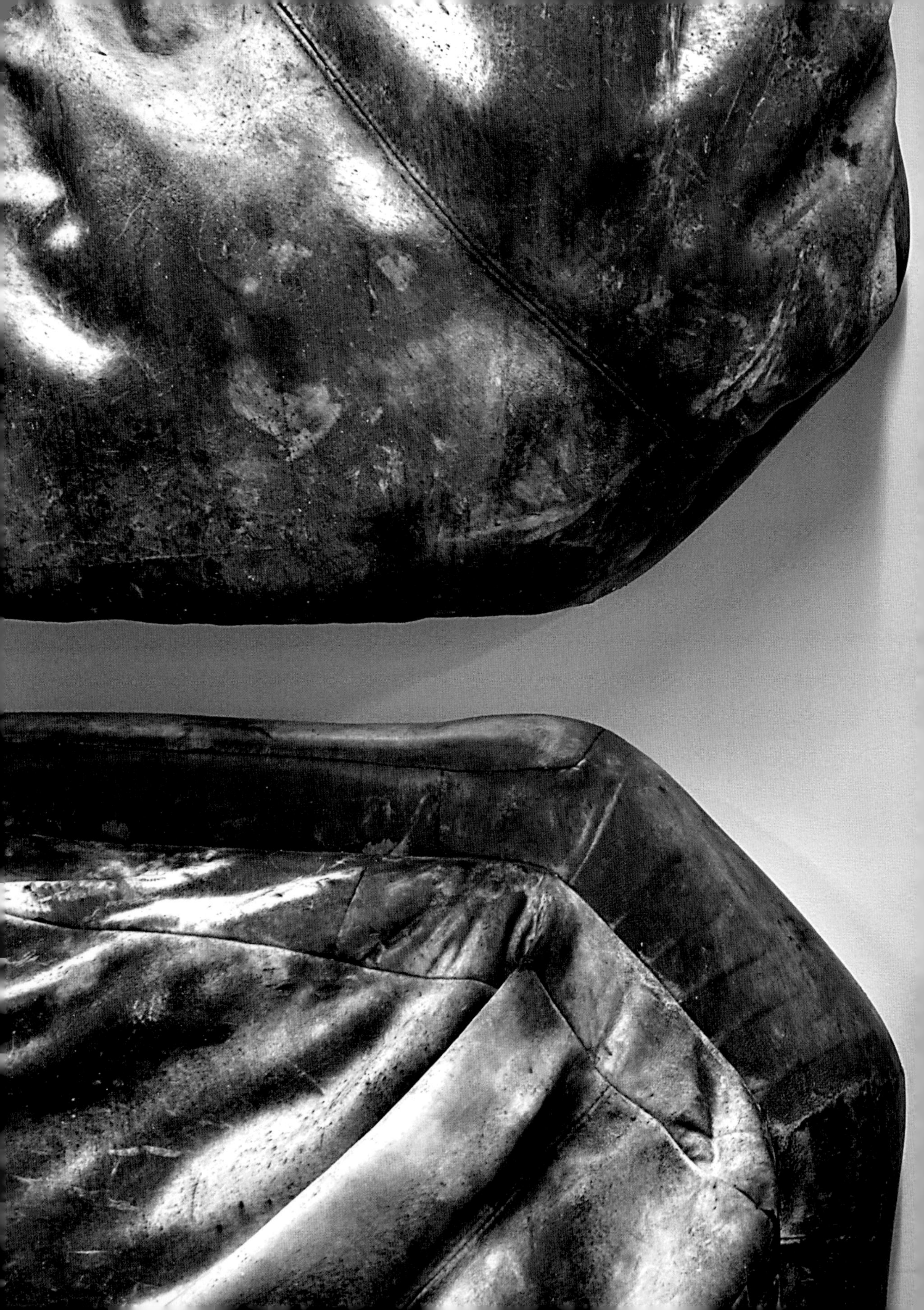

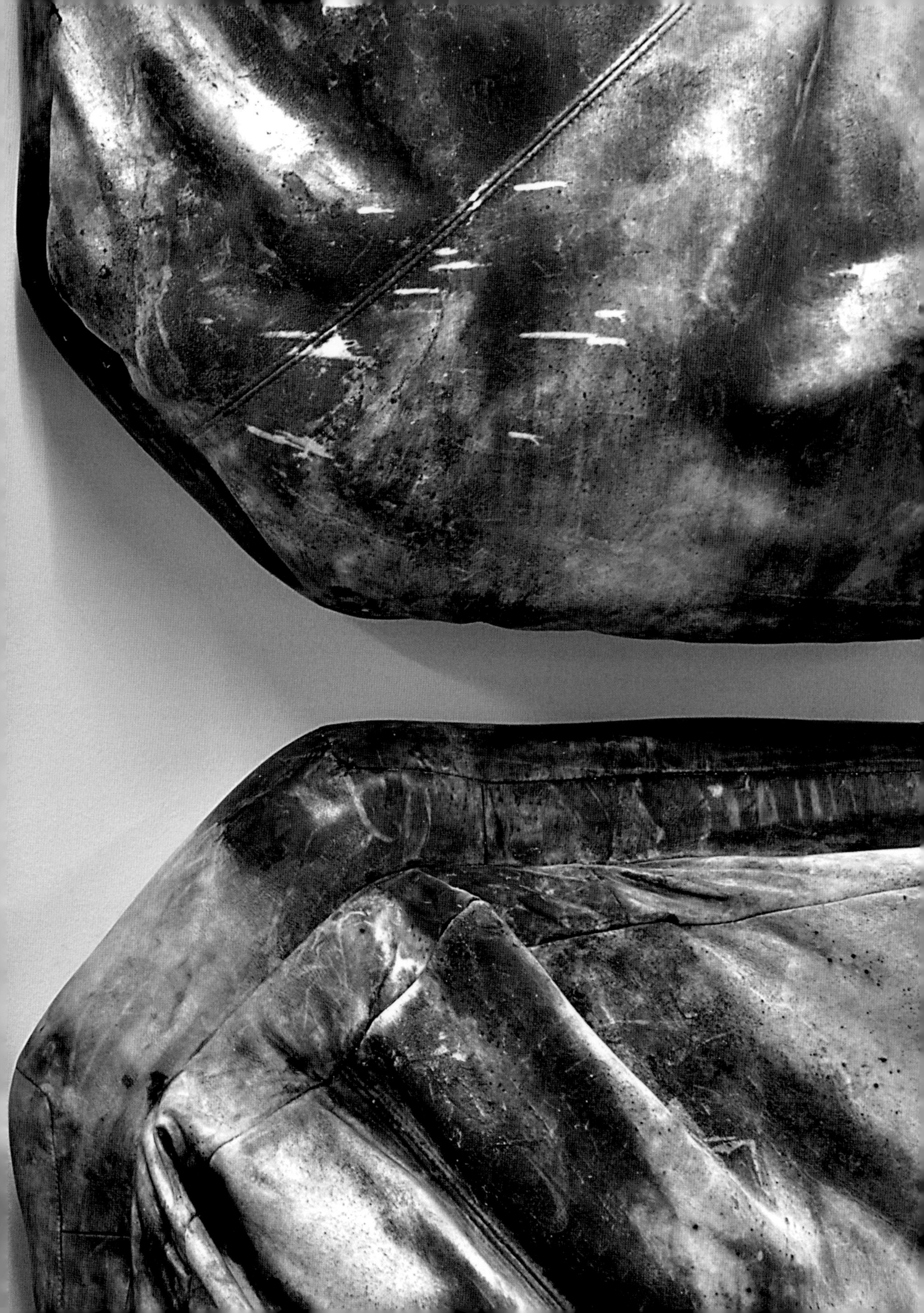

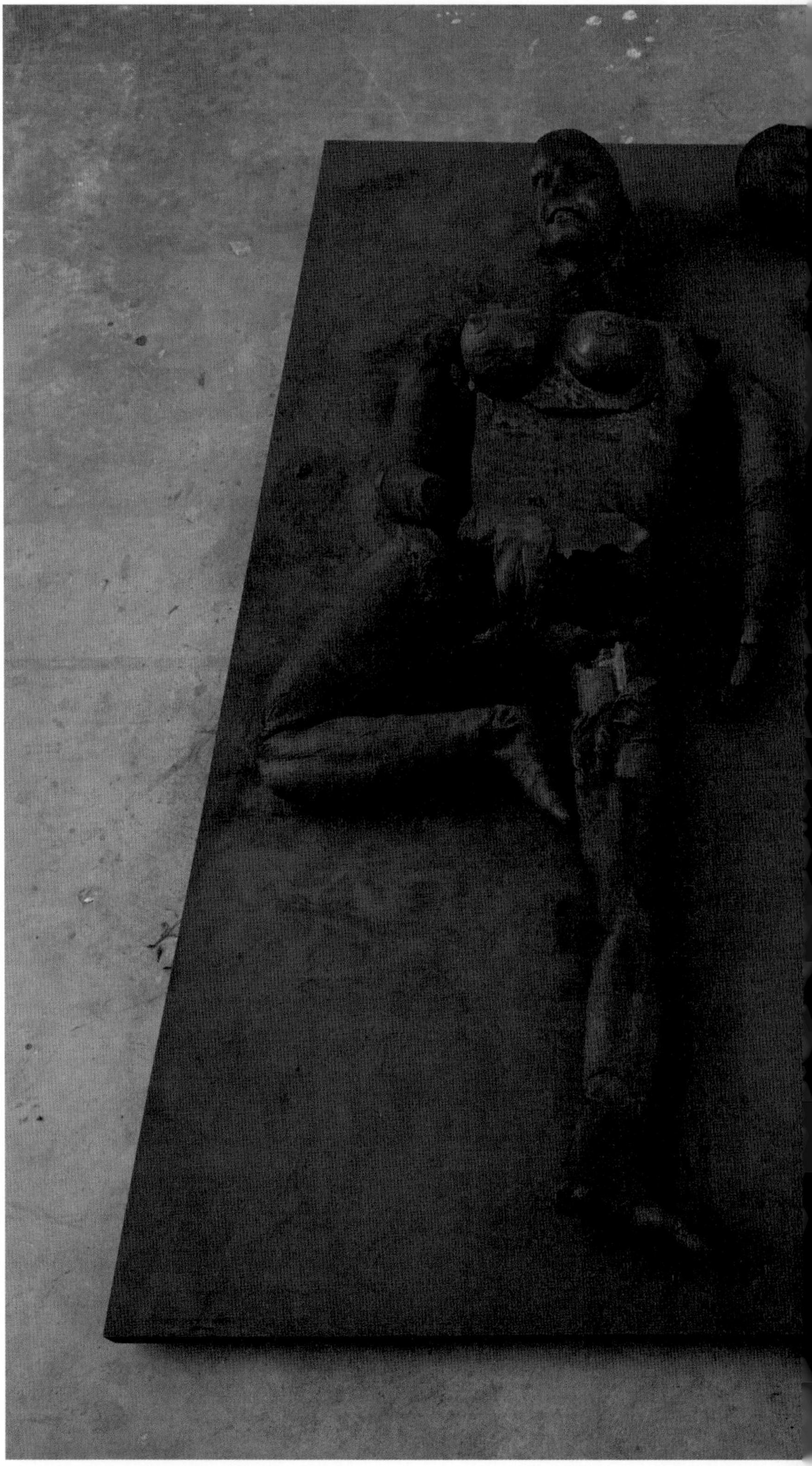

Dismembered/Remembered (Charcoal Figures), 2015

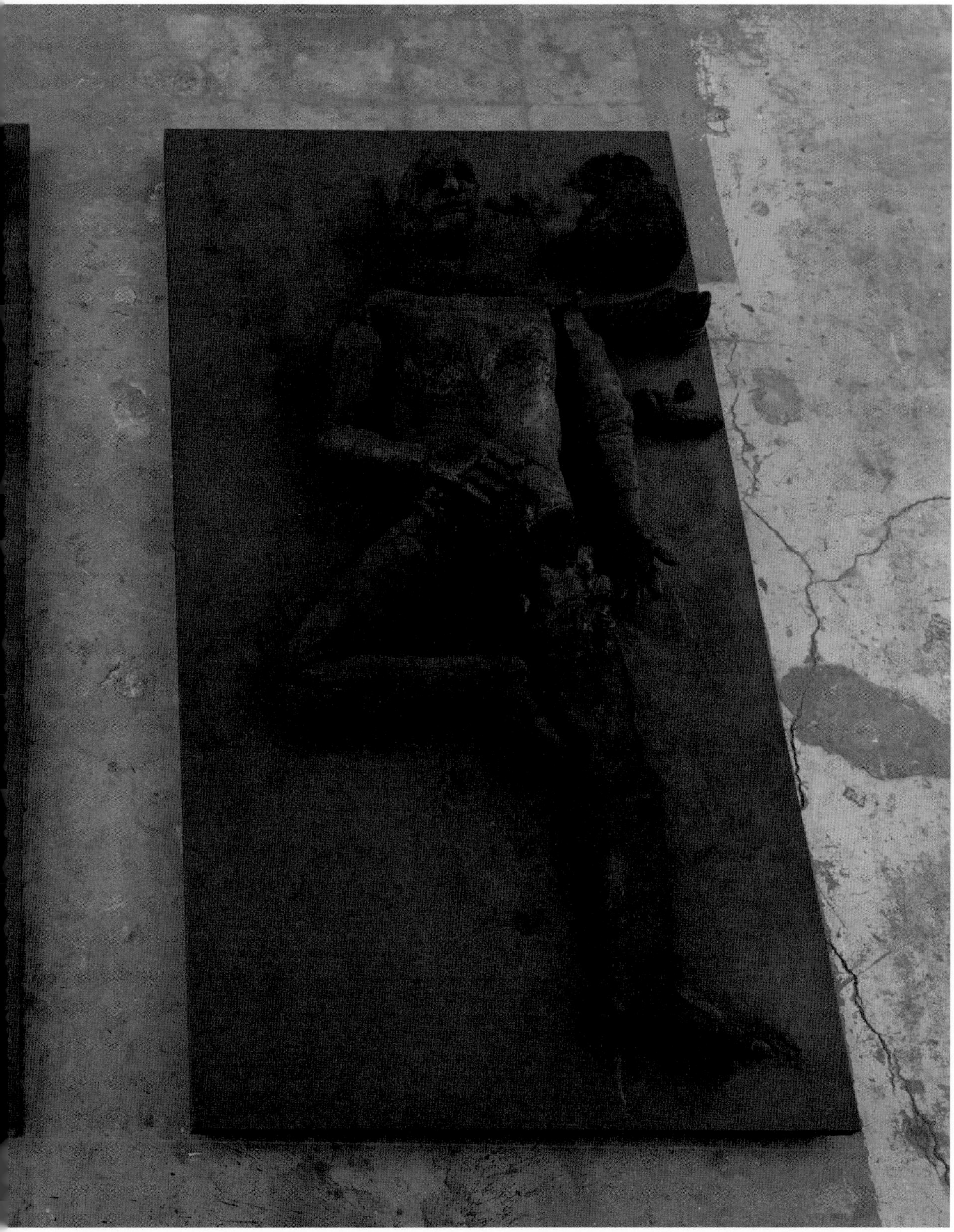

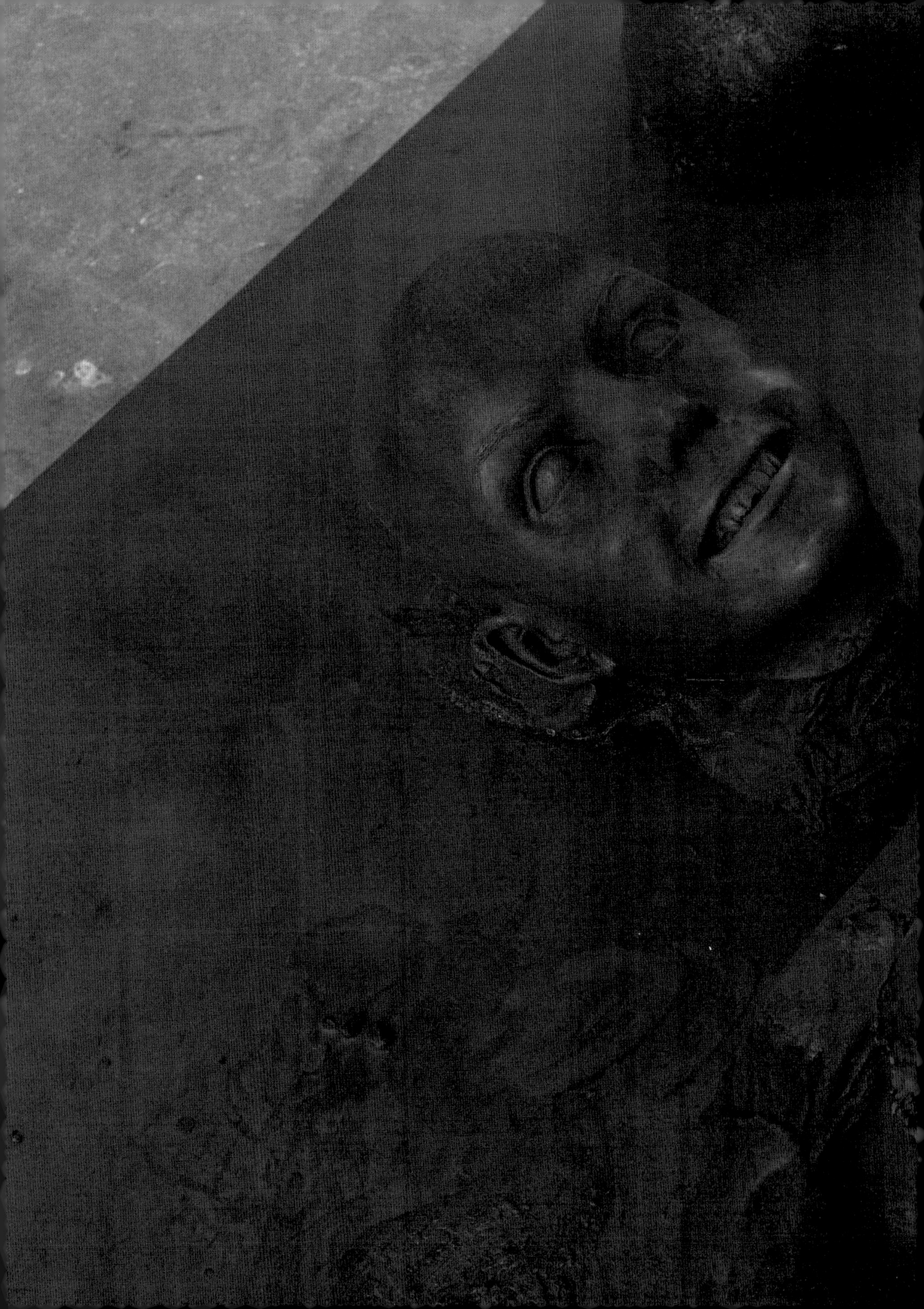

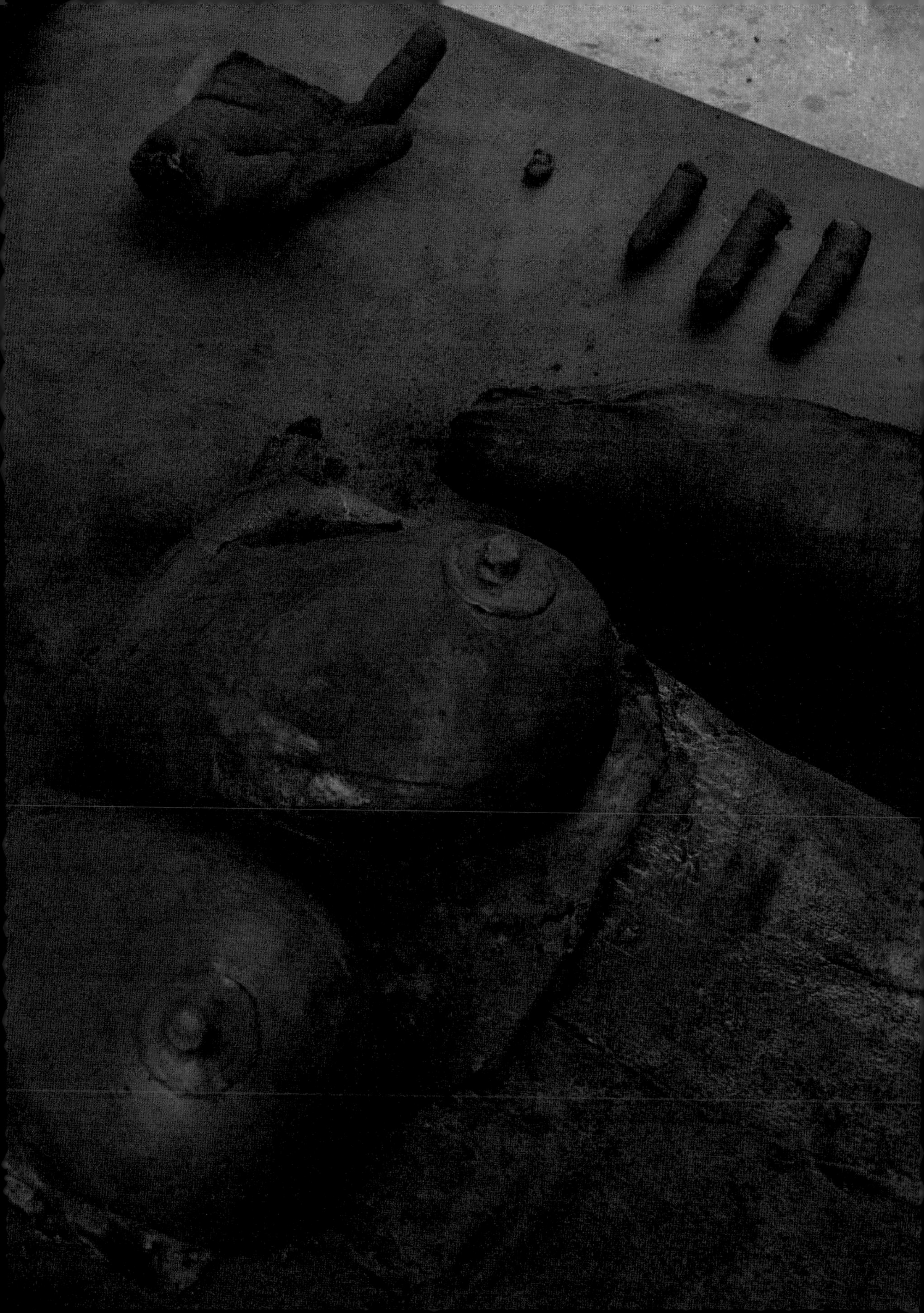

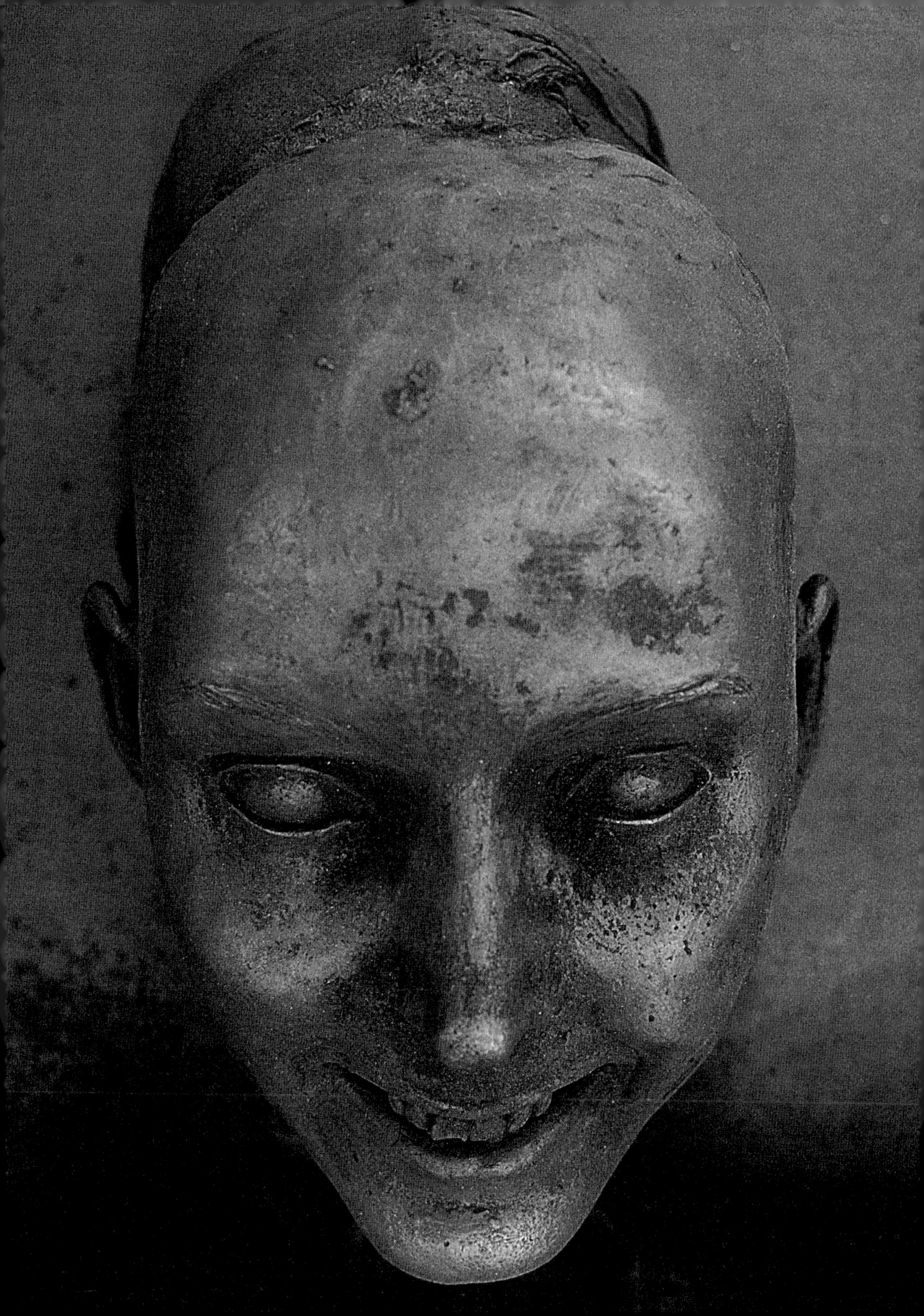

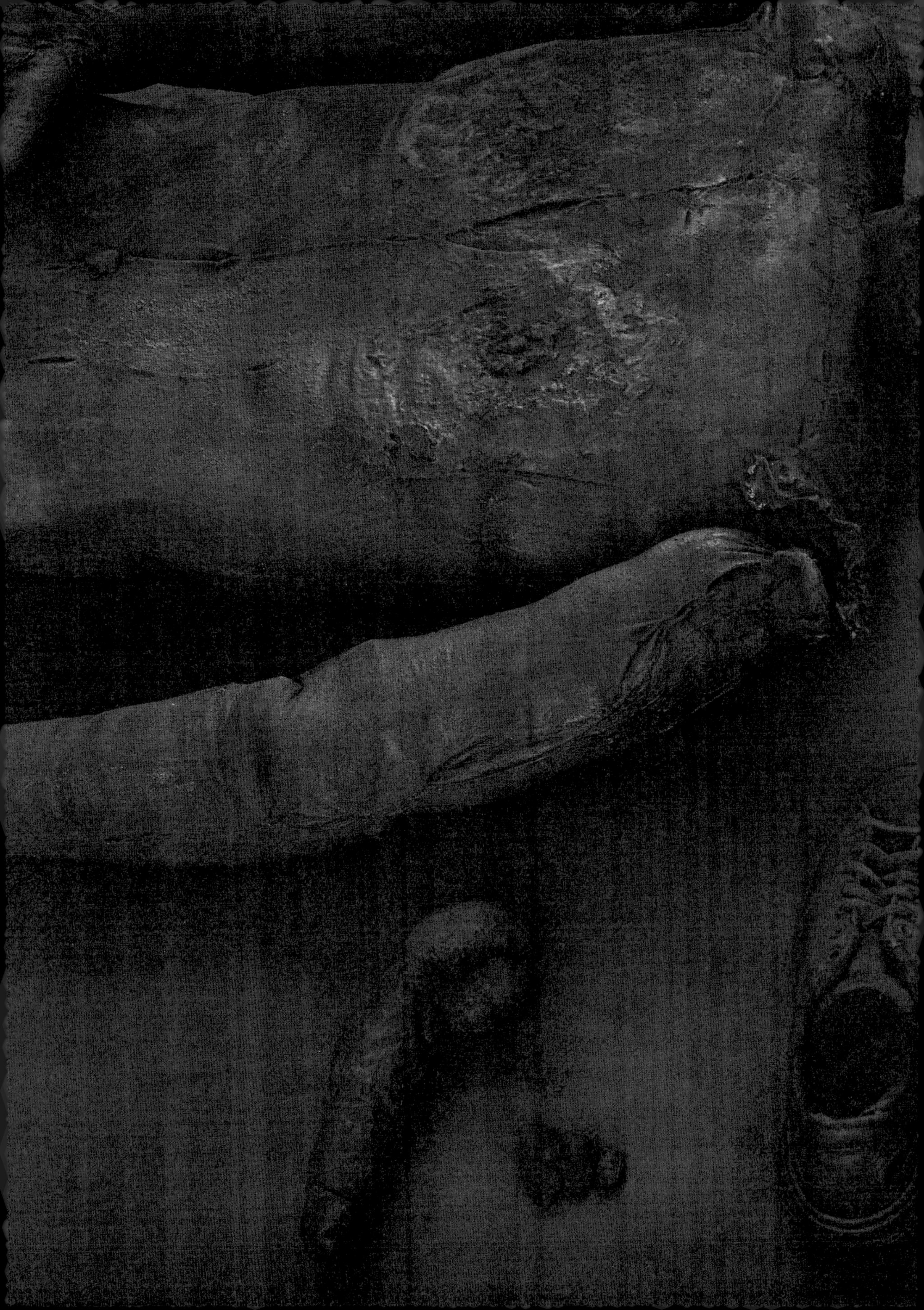

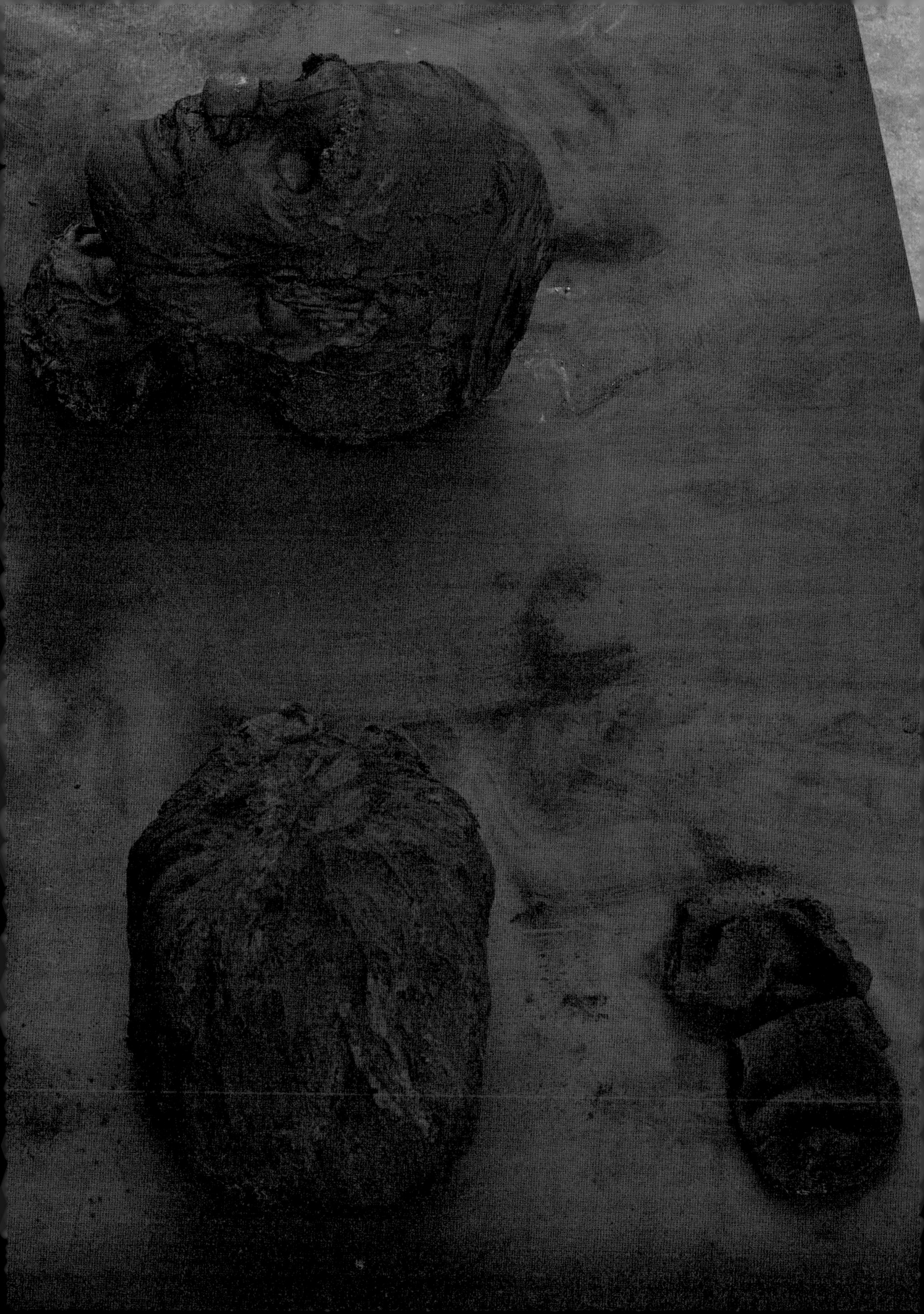

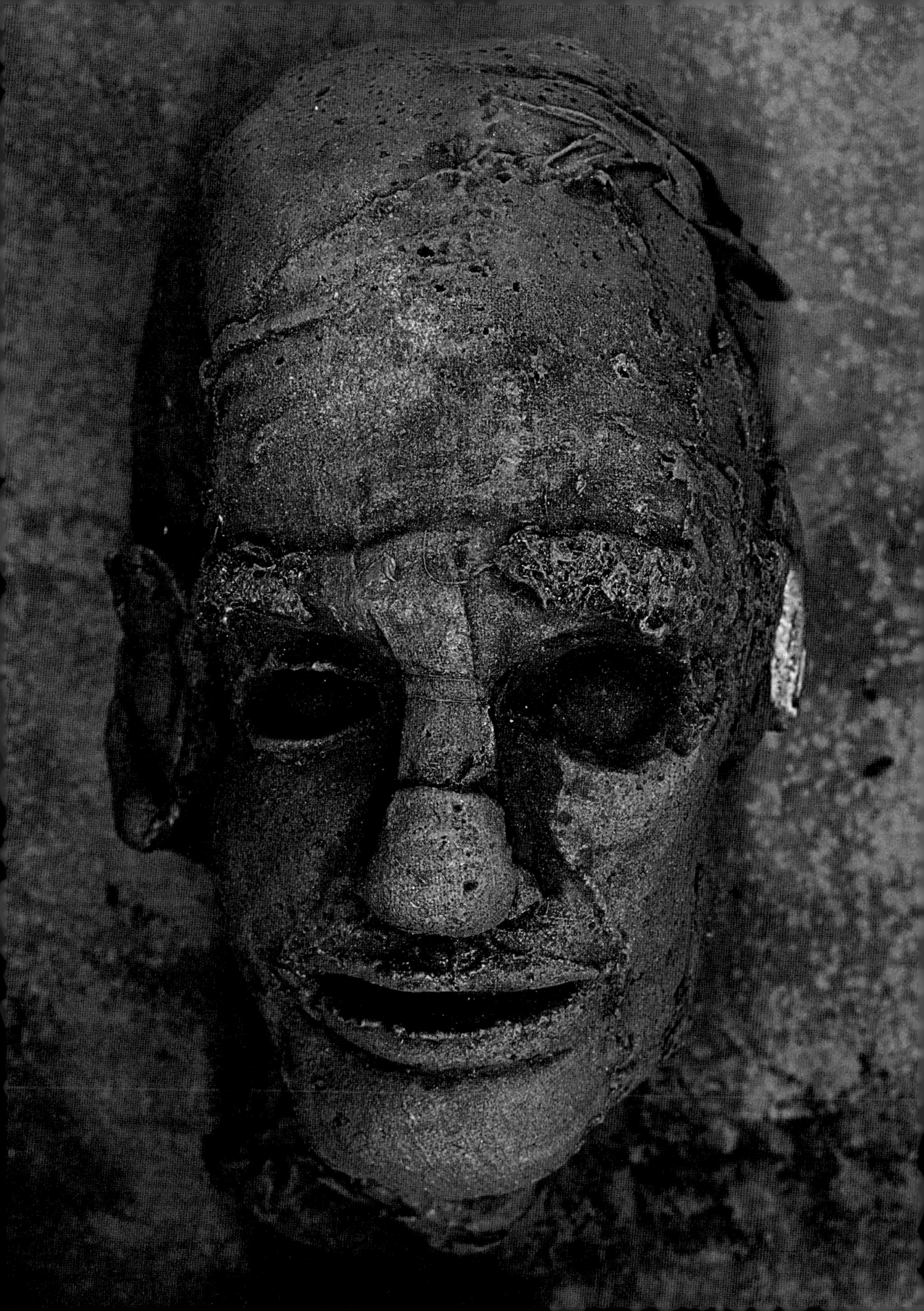

Untitled (1000 cans), 2015

Nutrition Facts

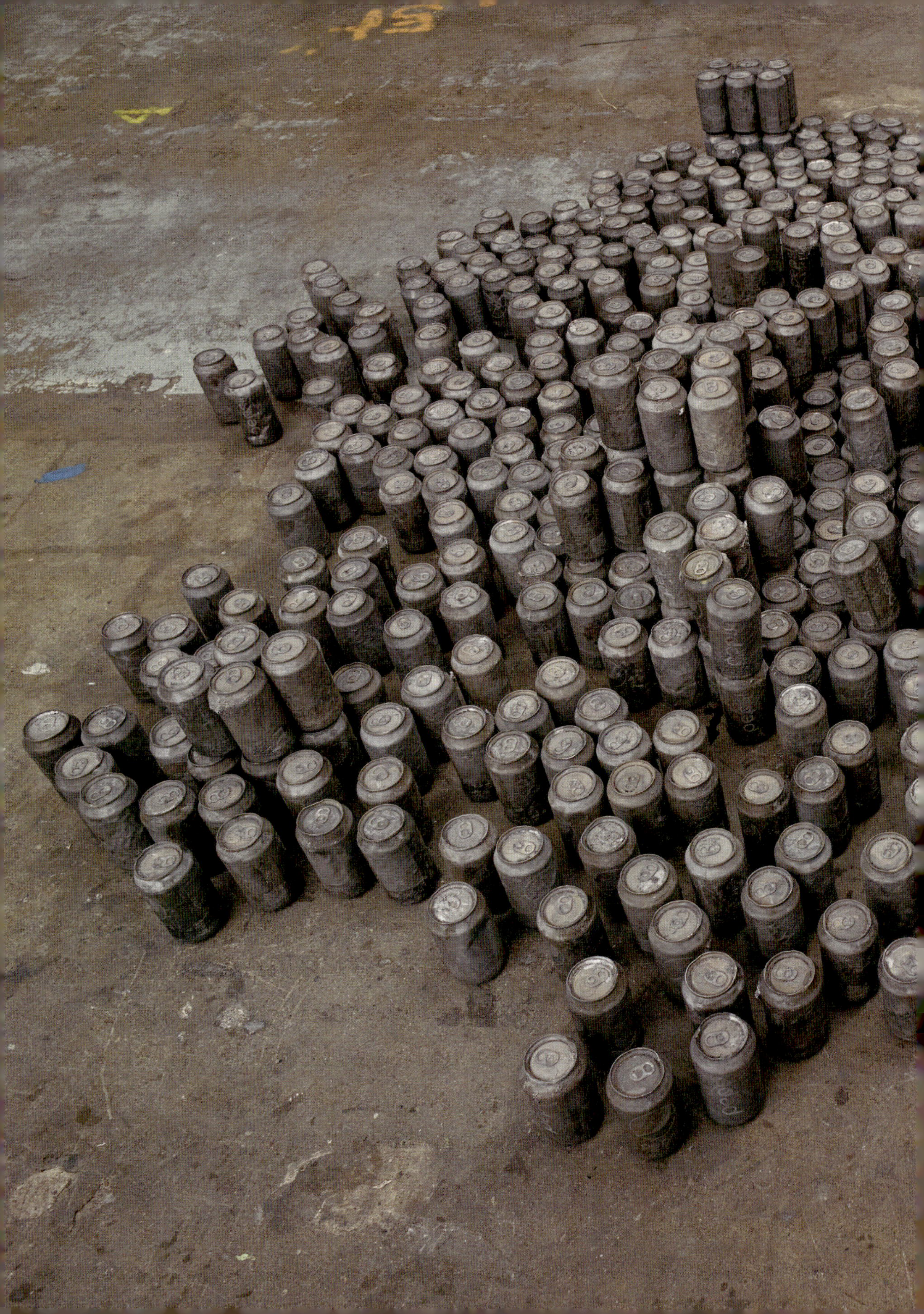

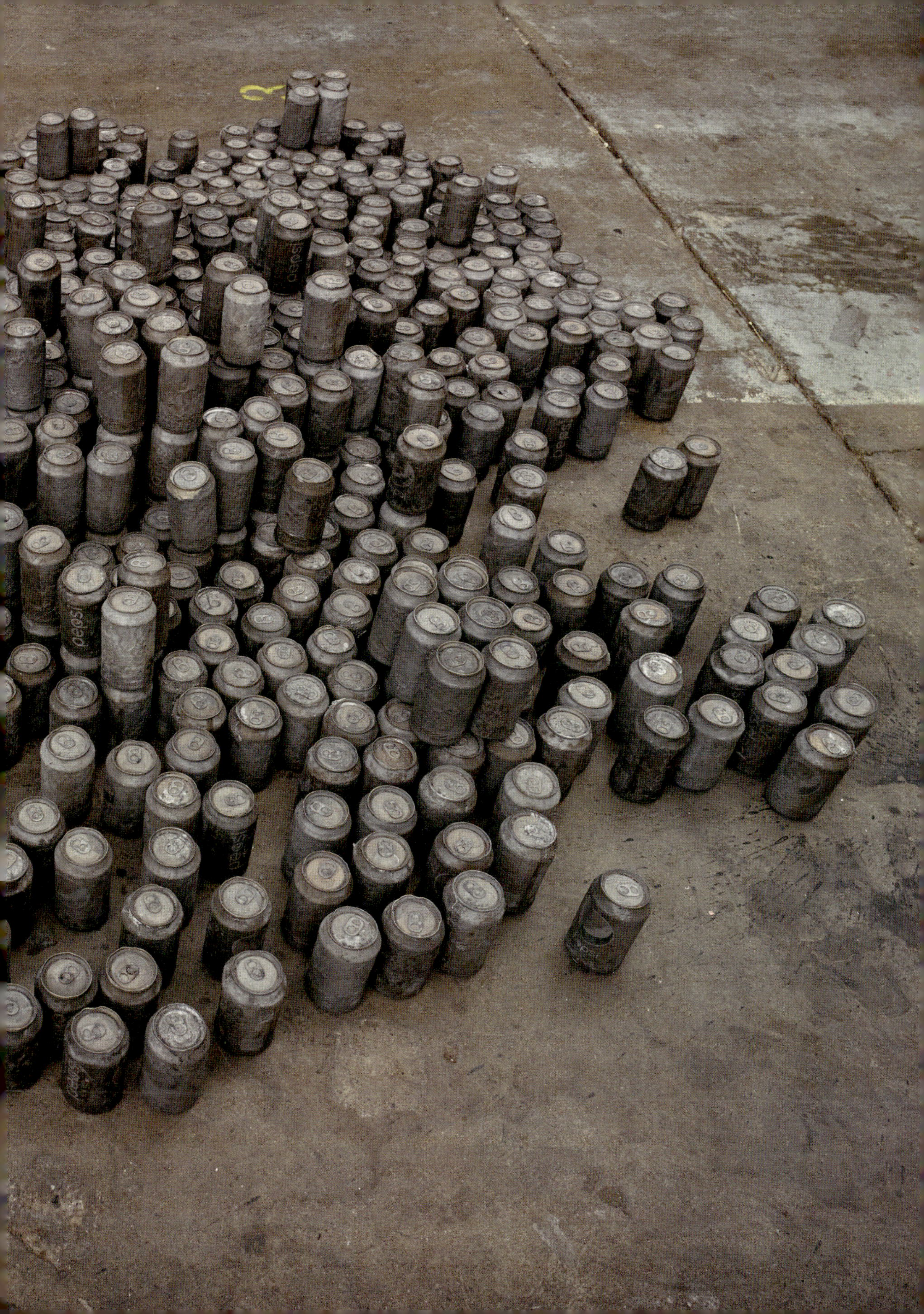

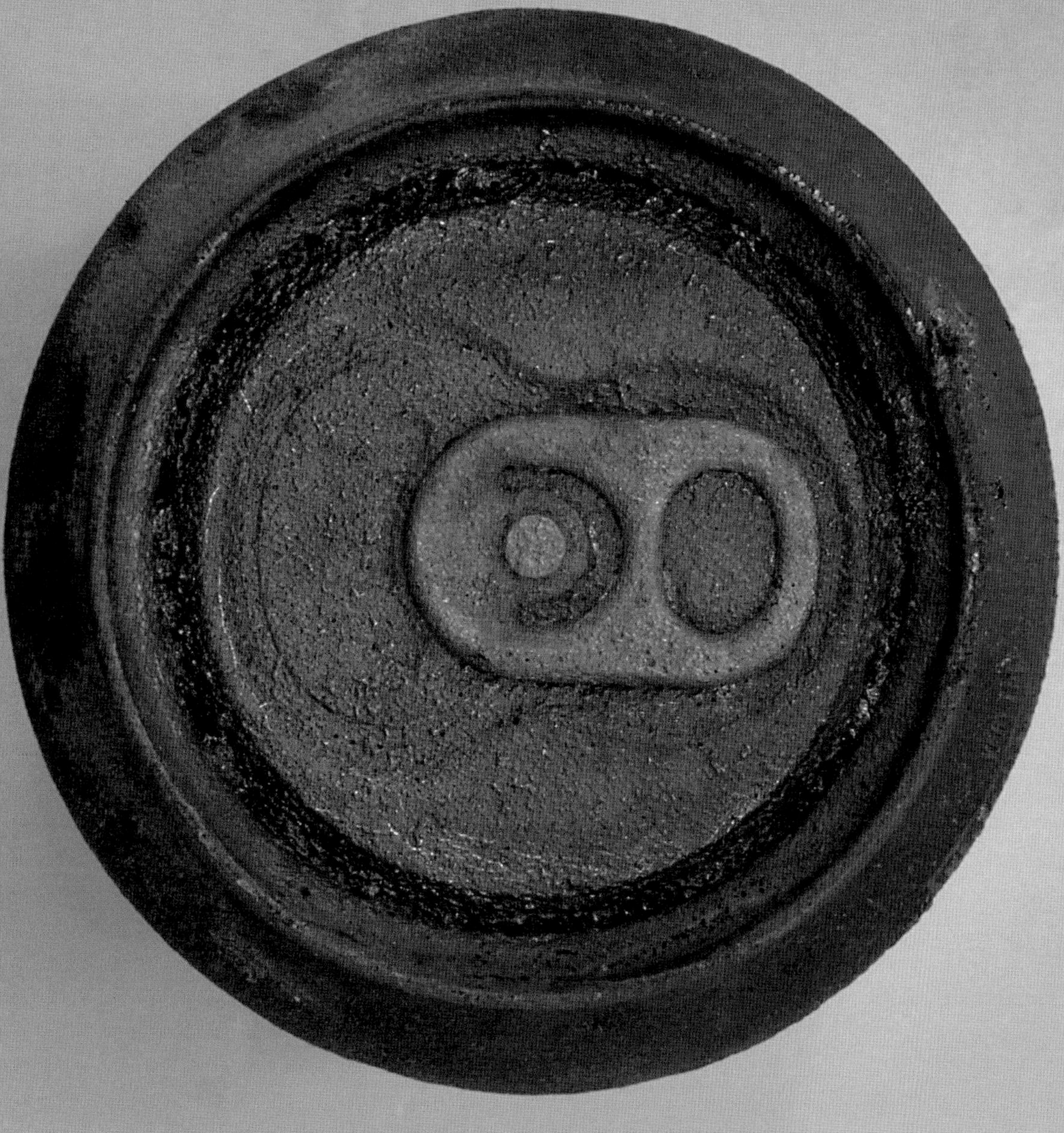

Brown Recluse, 2015

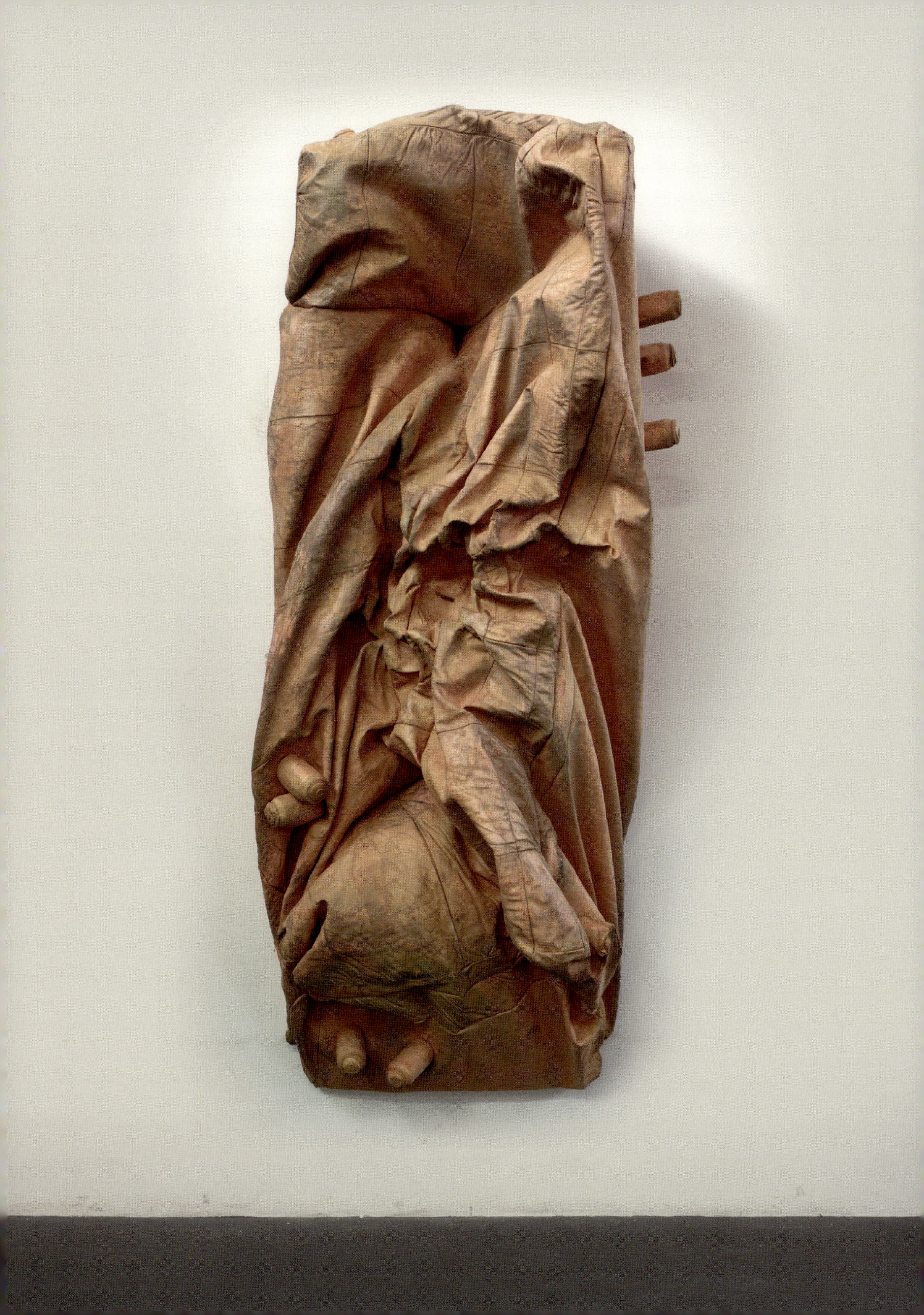

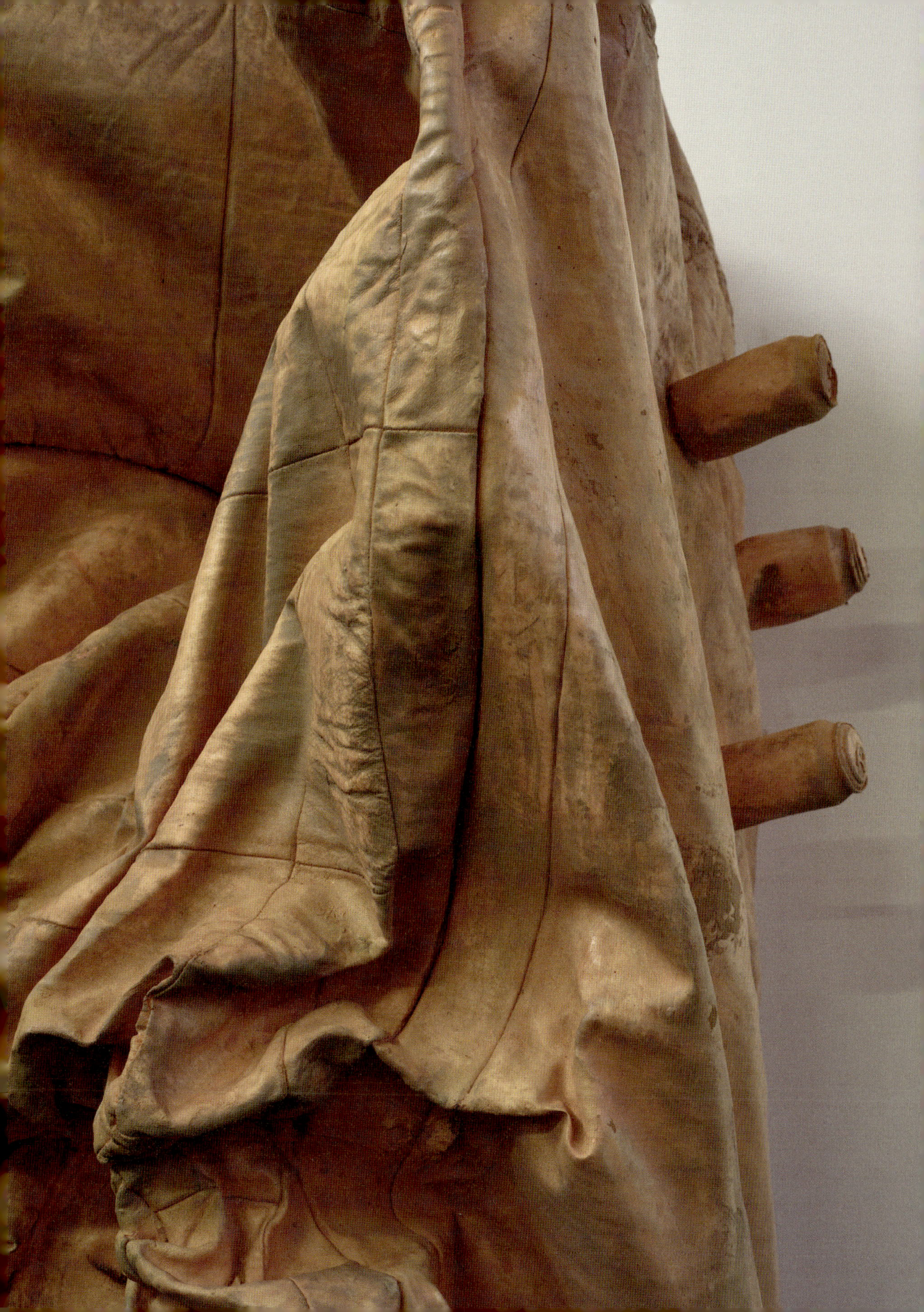

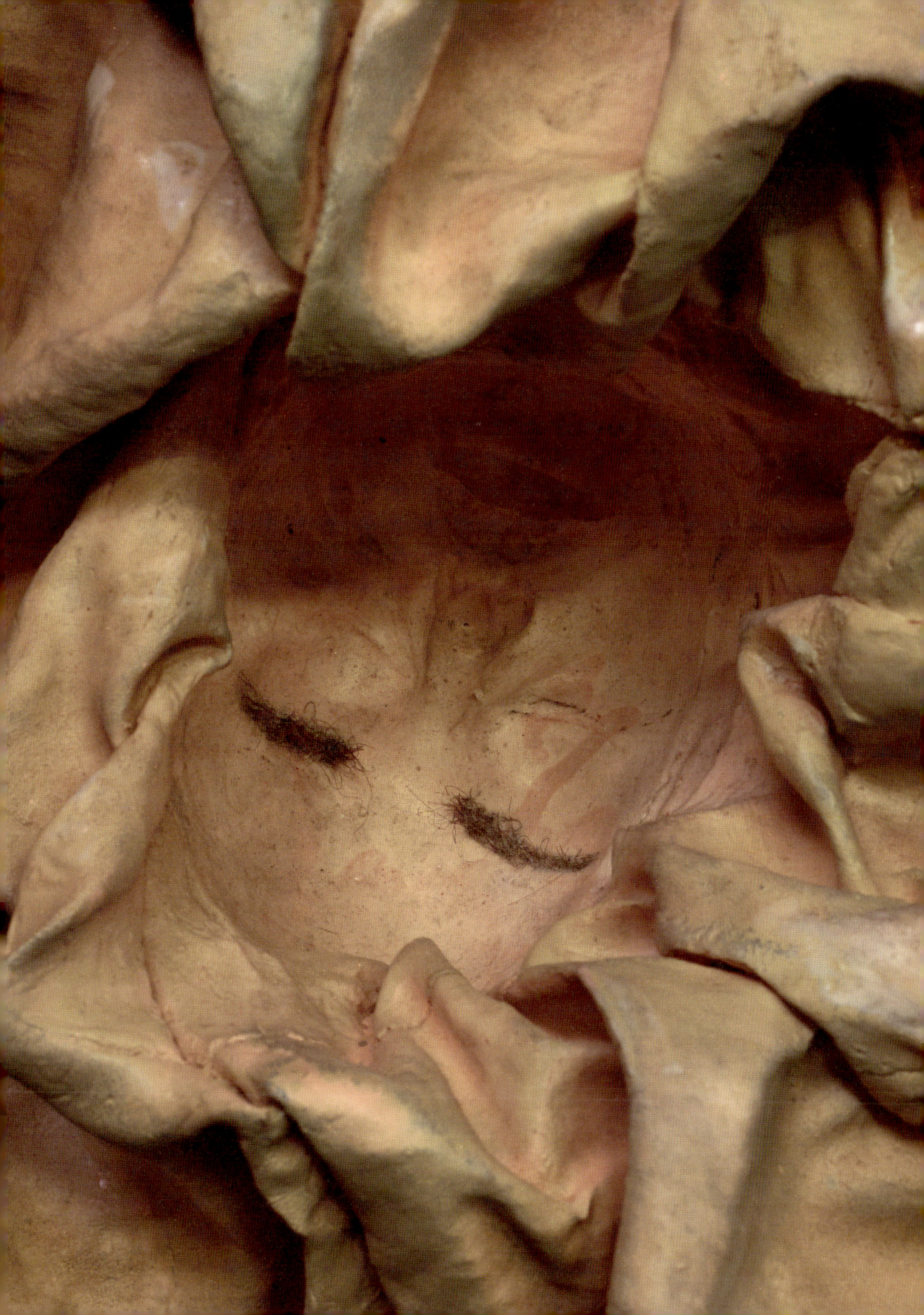

12:43 A.M., 2015

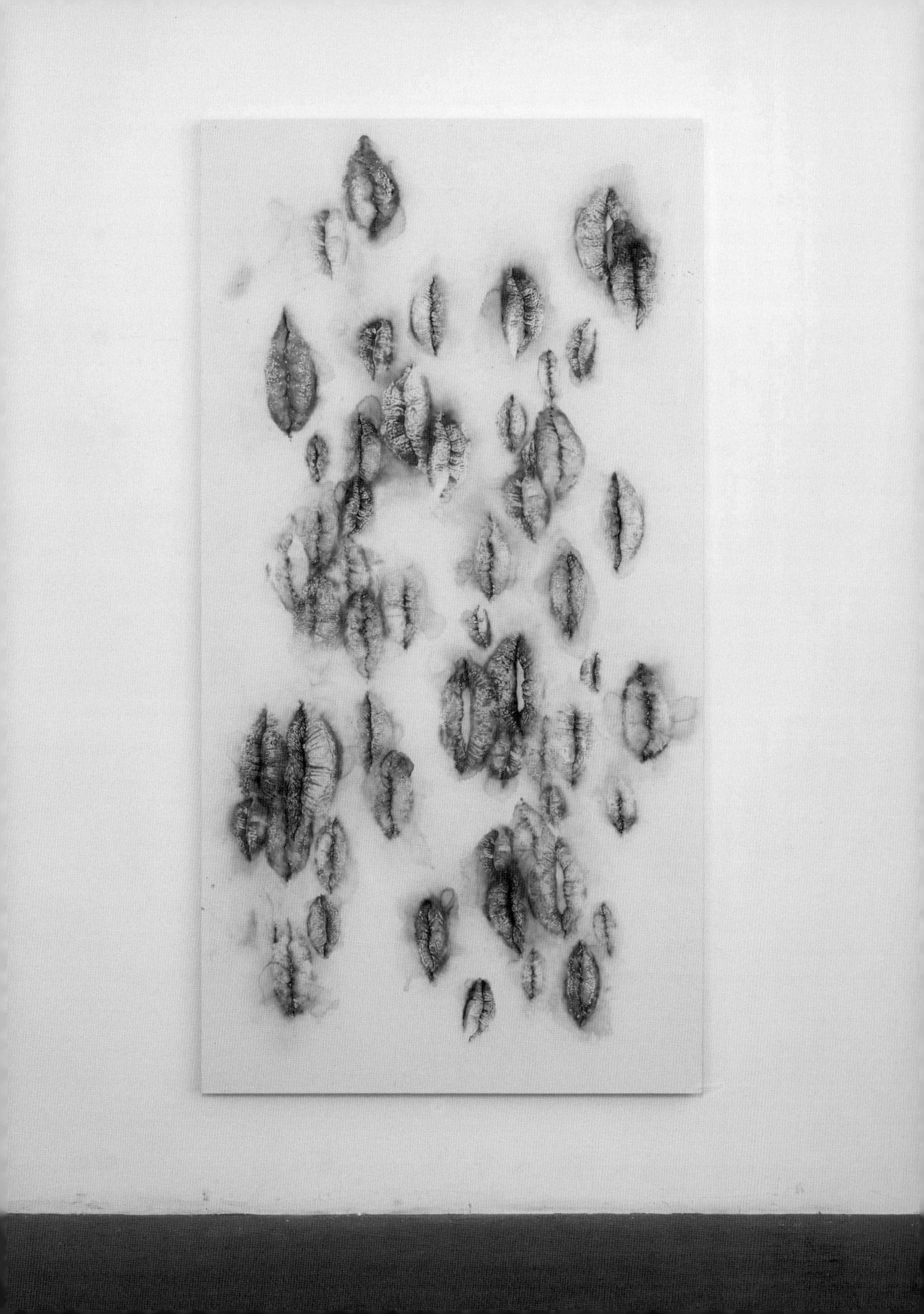

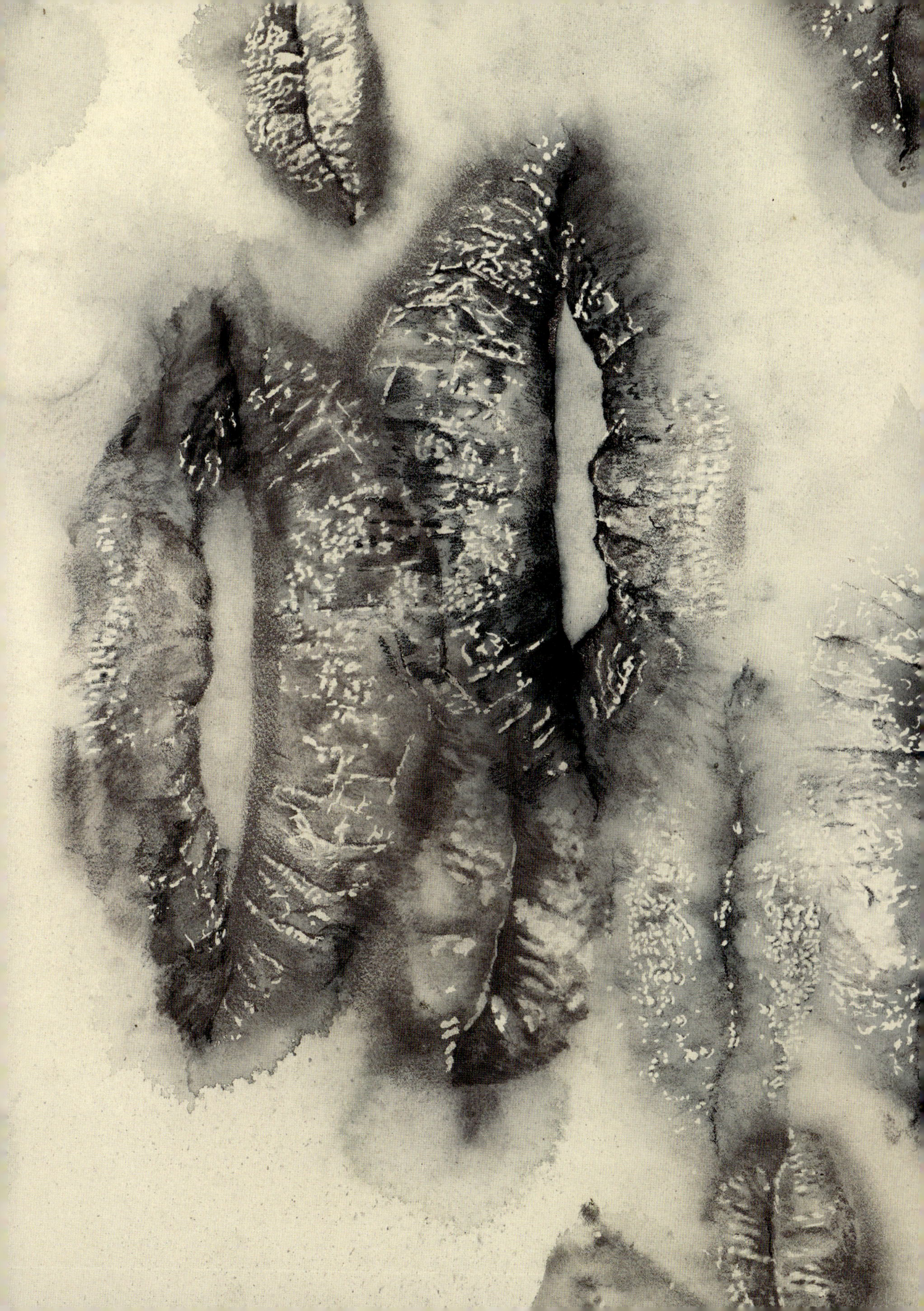

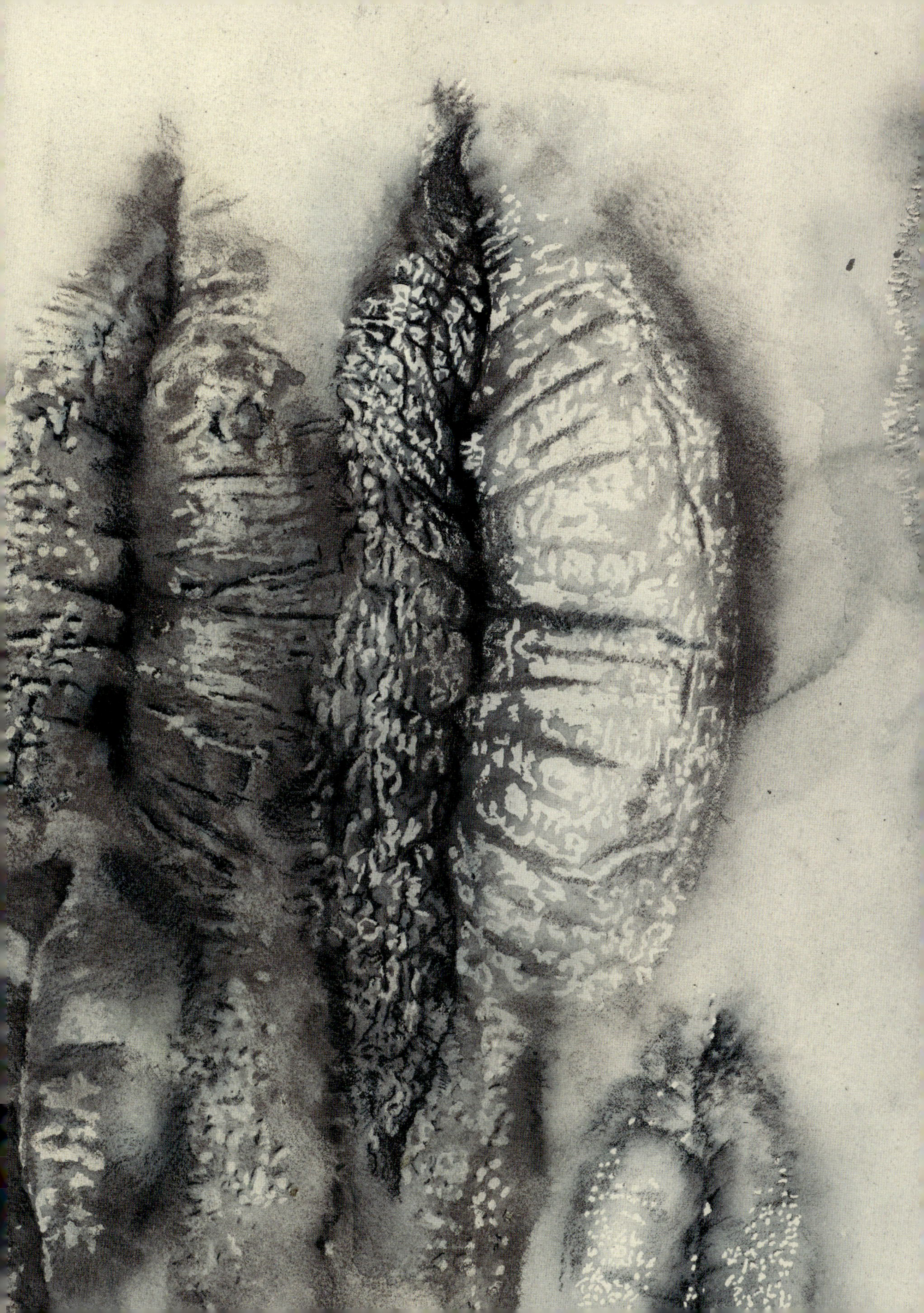

Death Bed, 2015

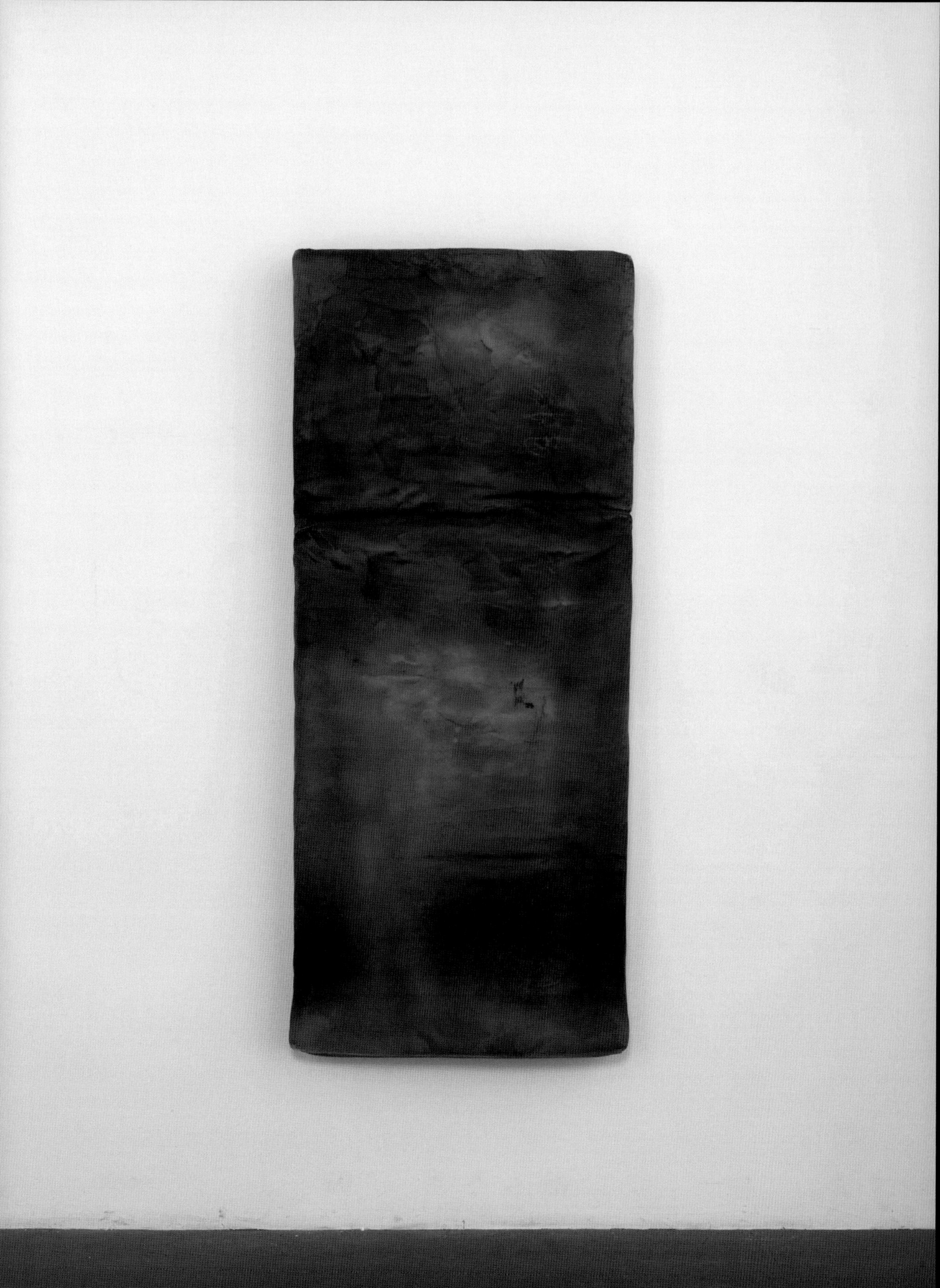

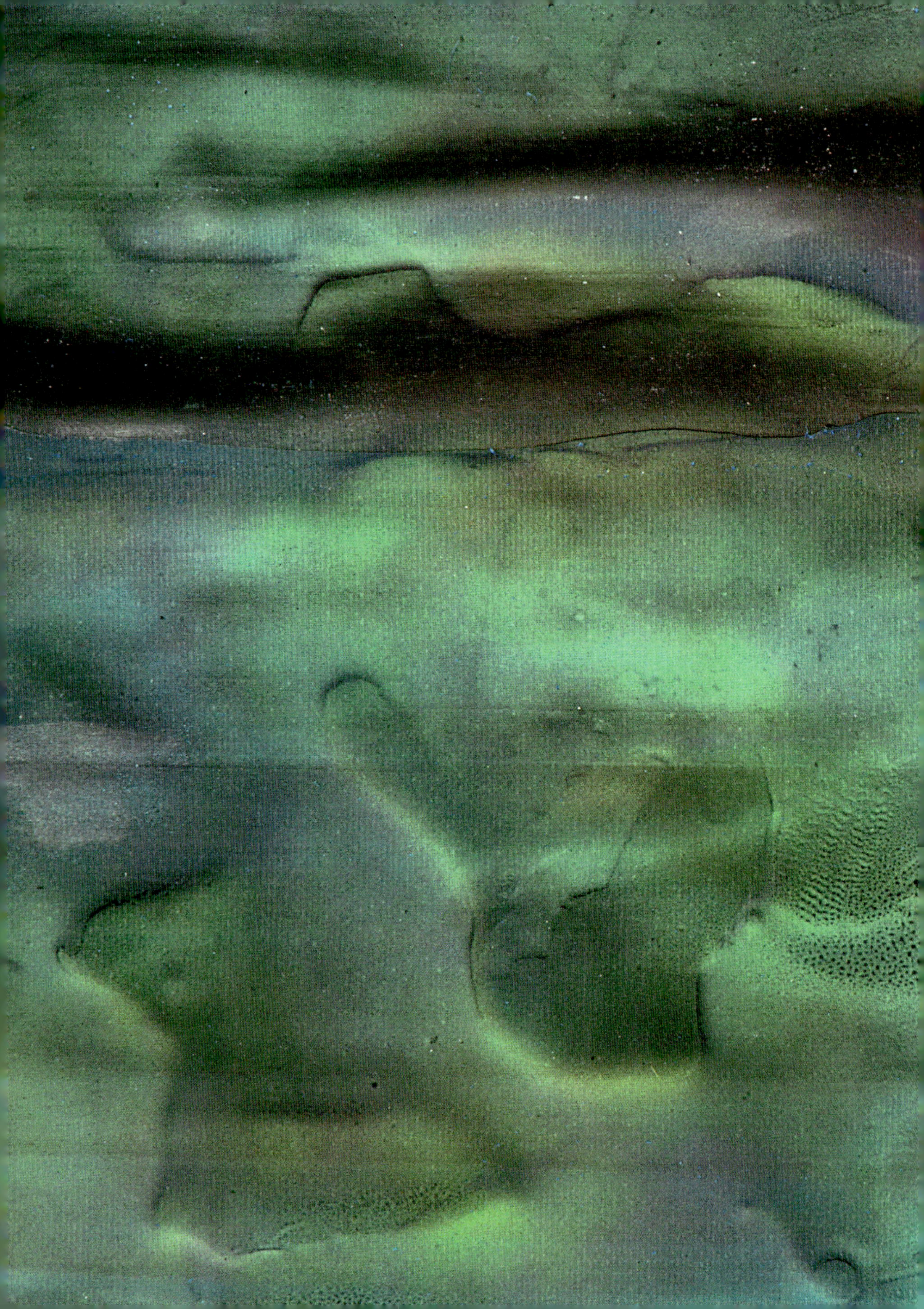

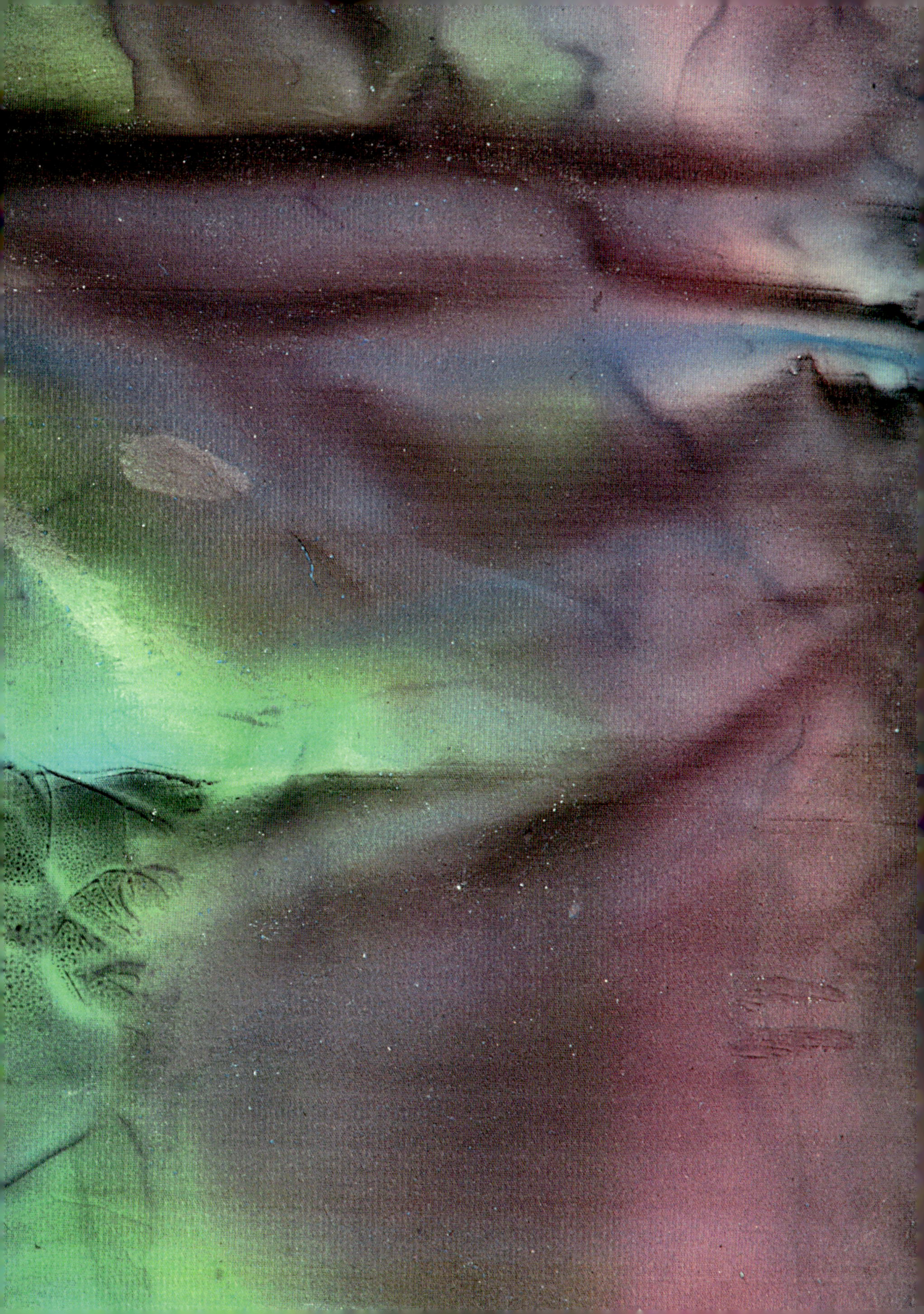

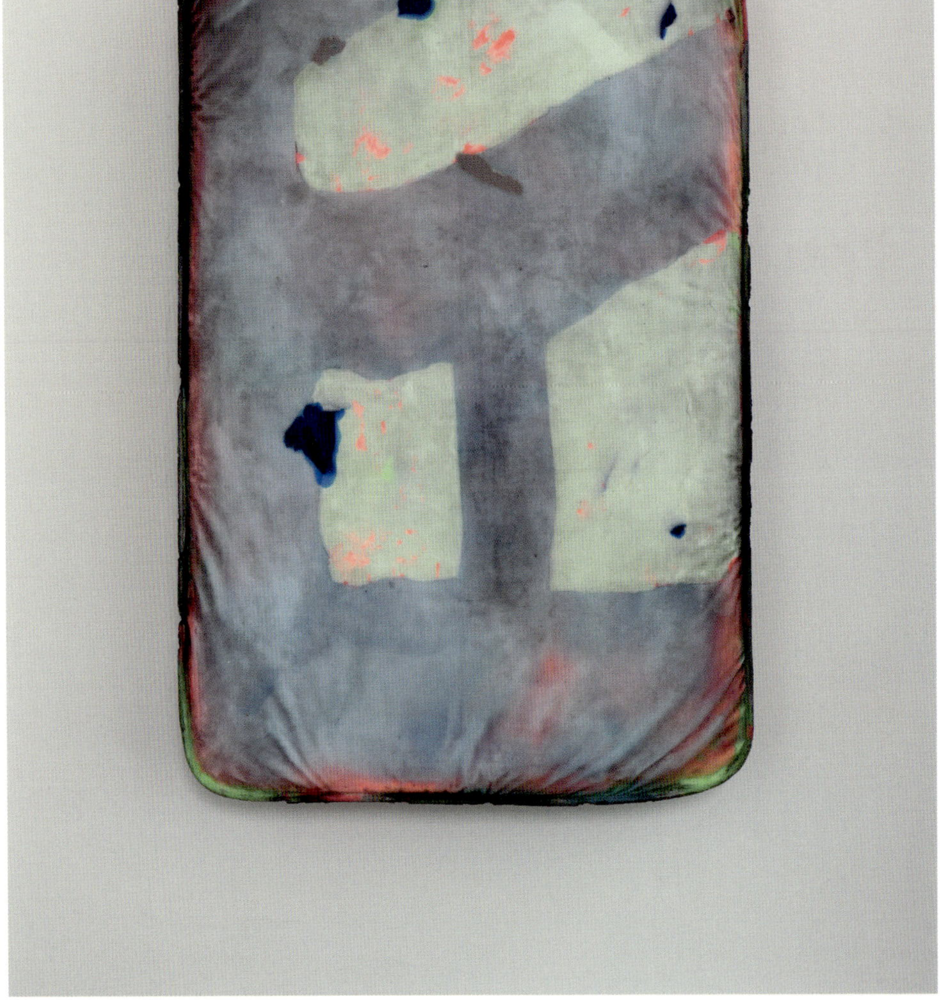

Crib Diptych, 2015

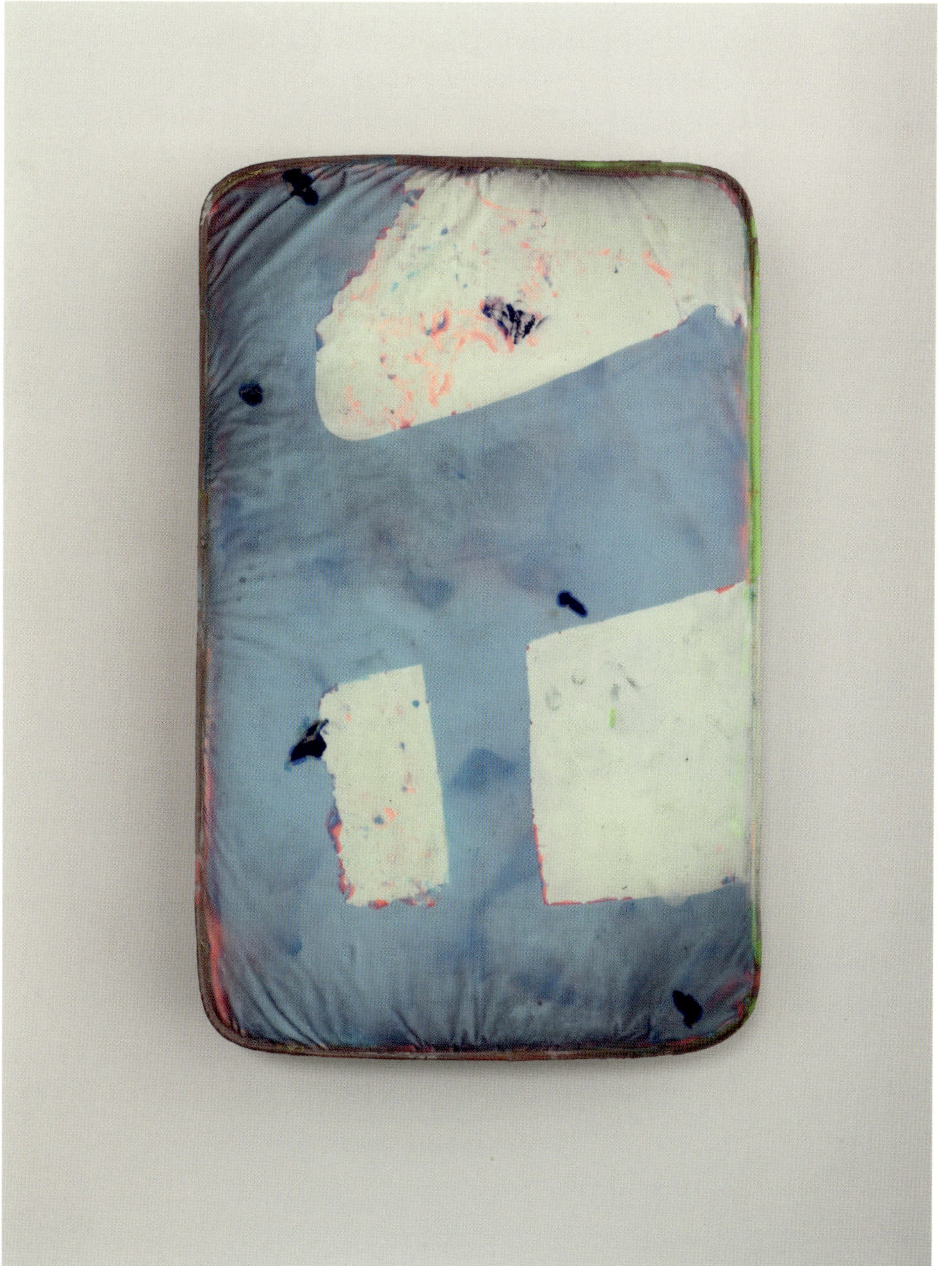

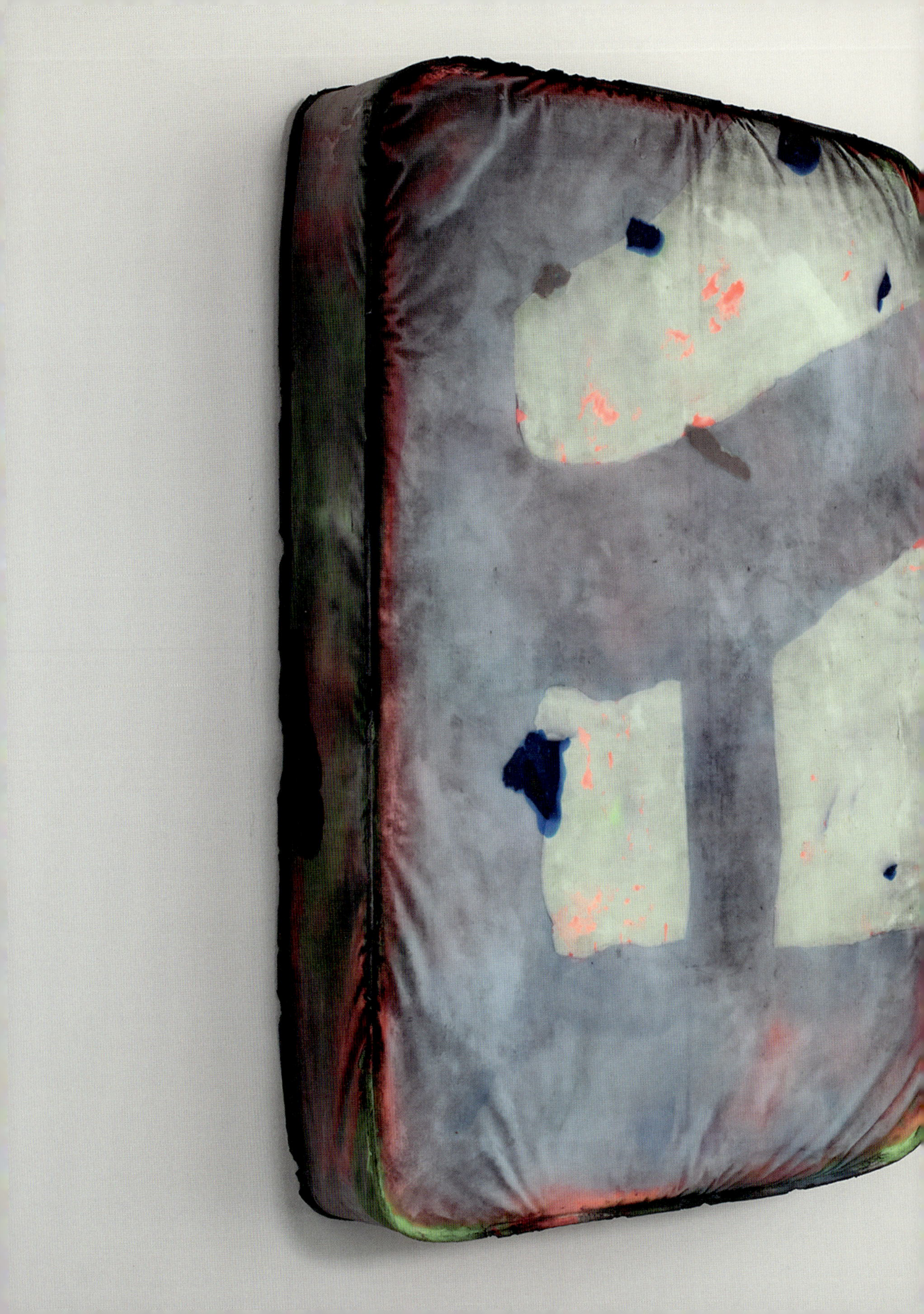

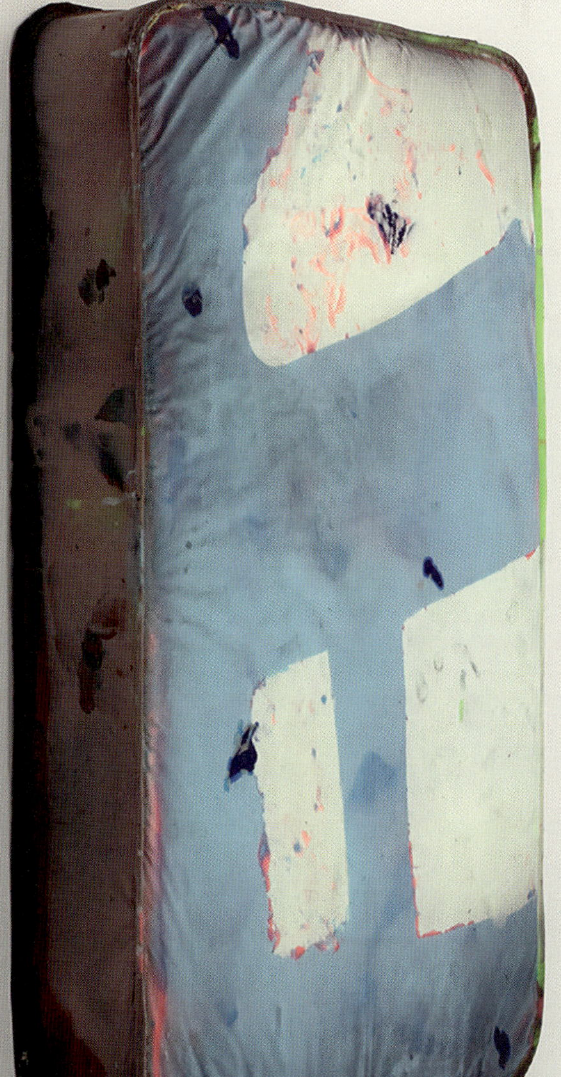

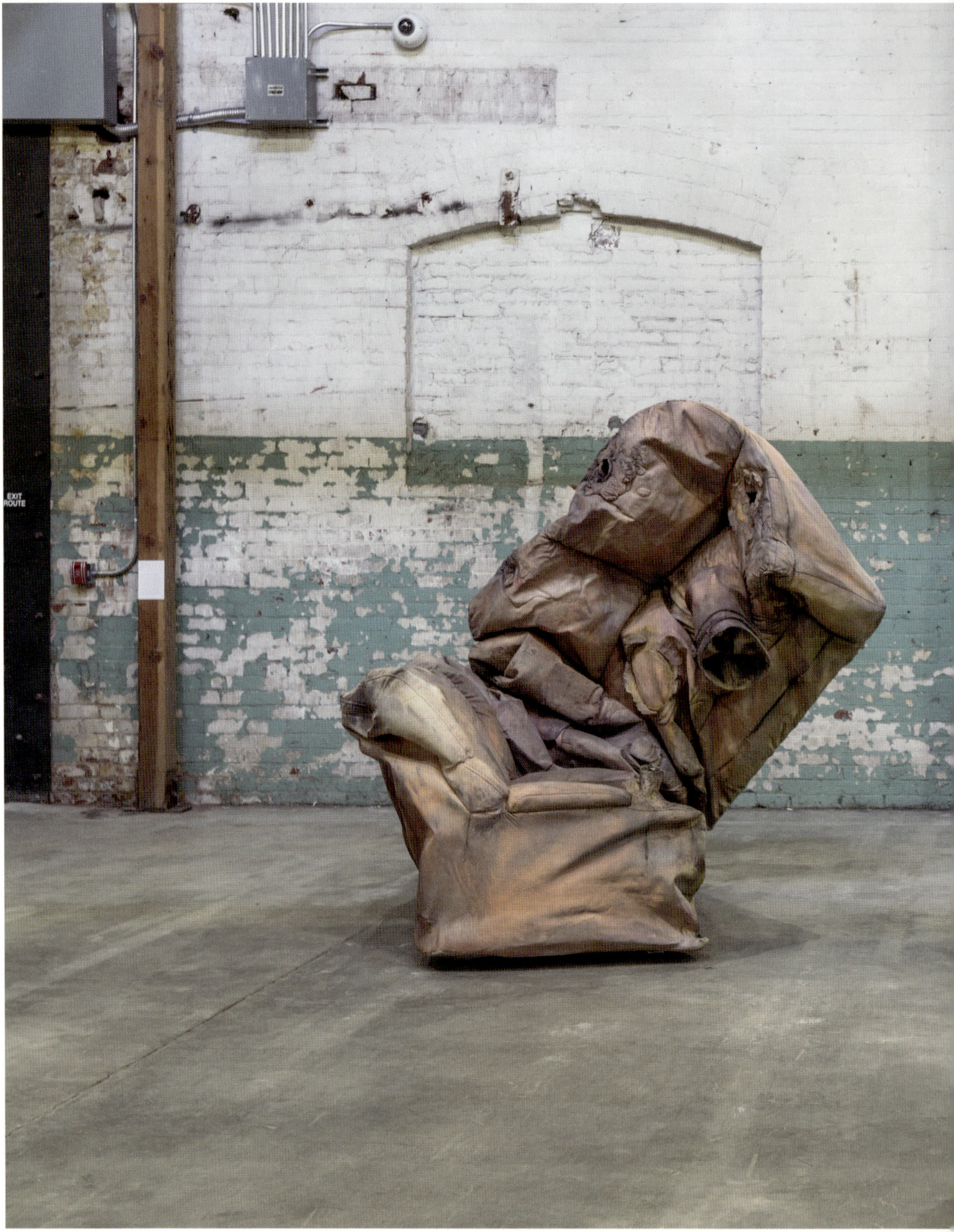

Left Brace Erase, Back Brace Face, 2016

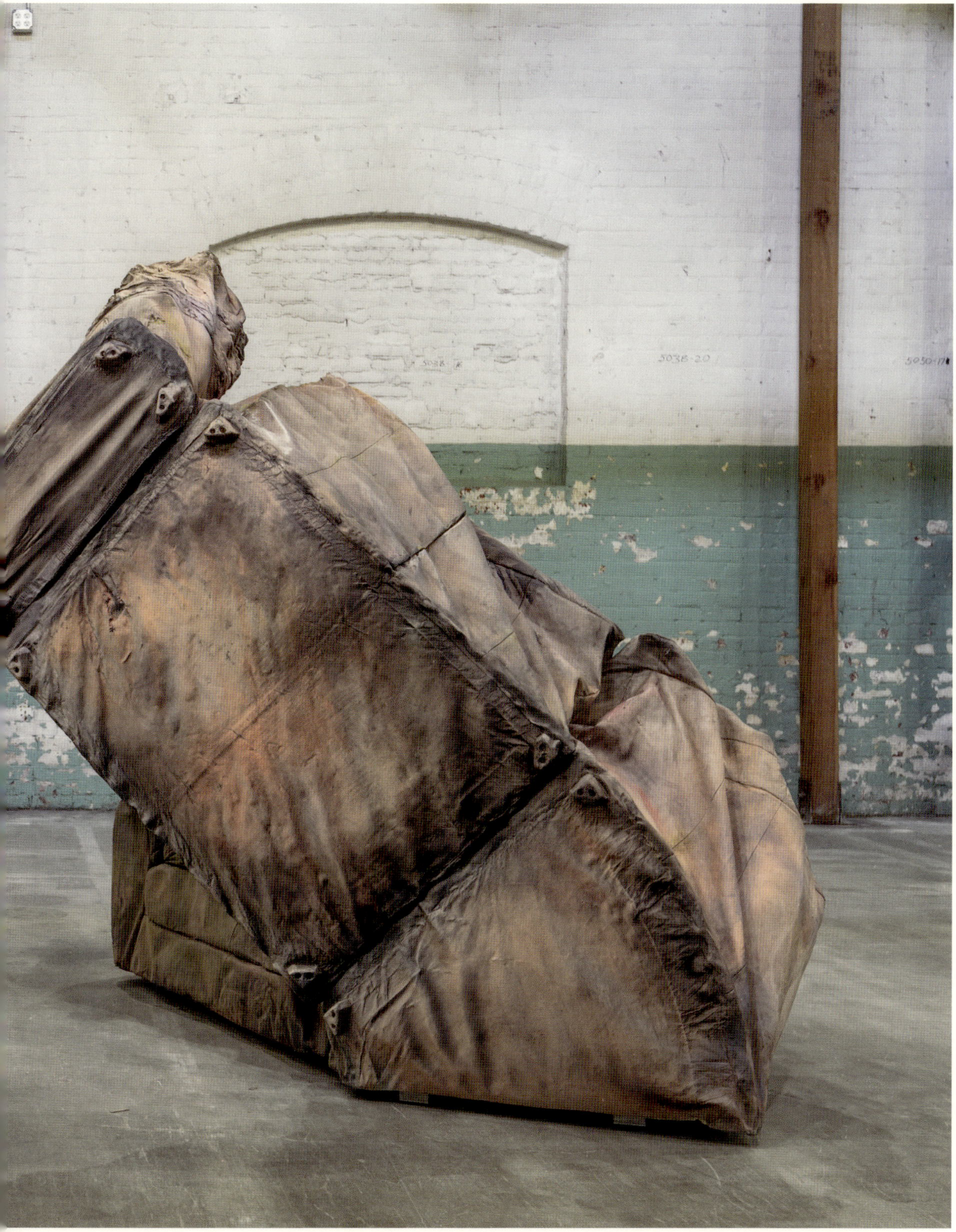

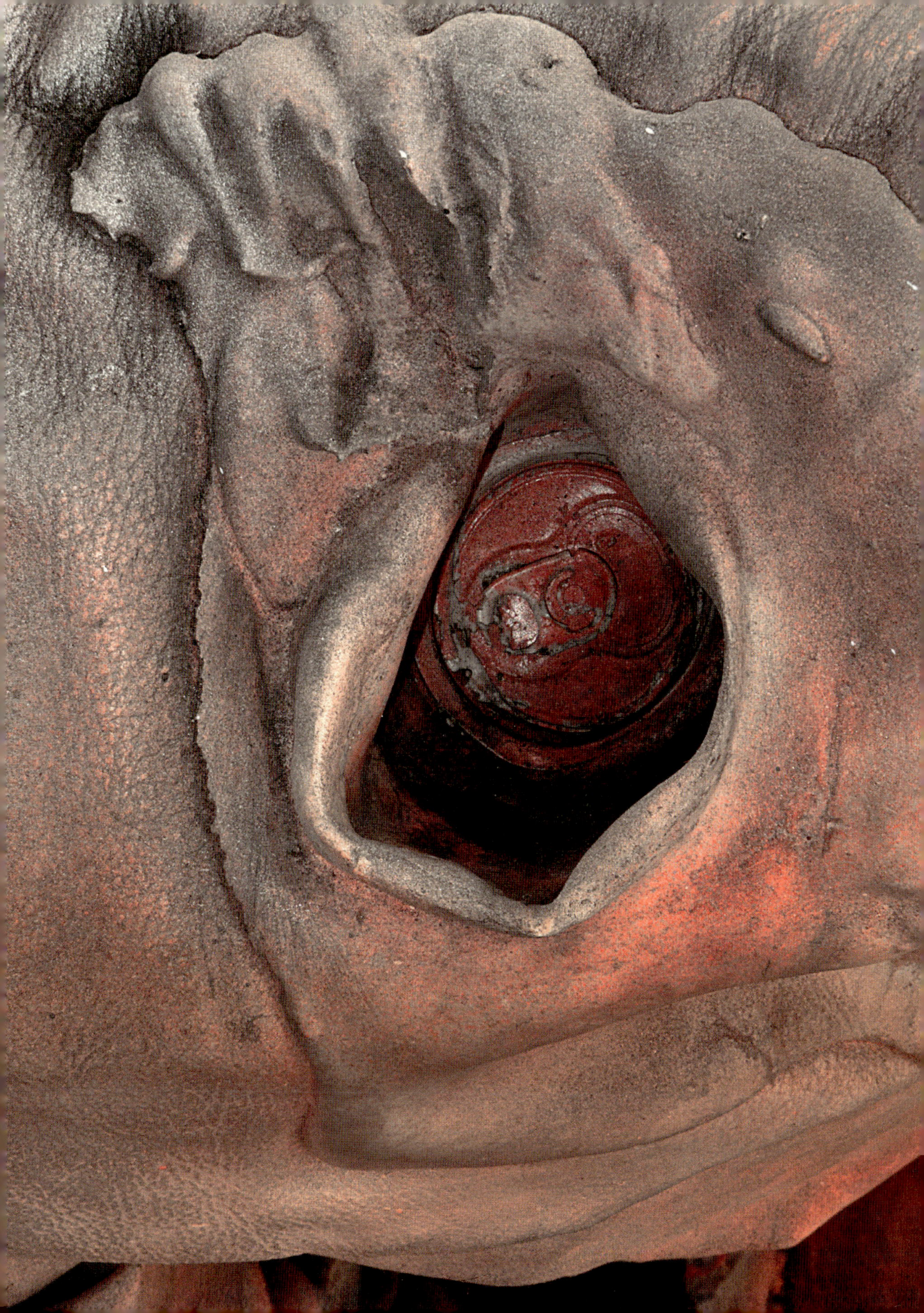

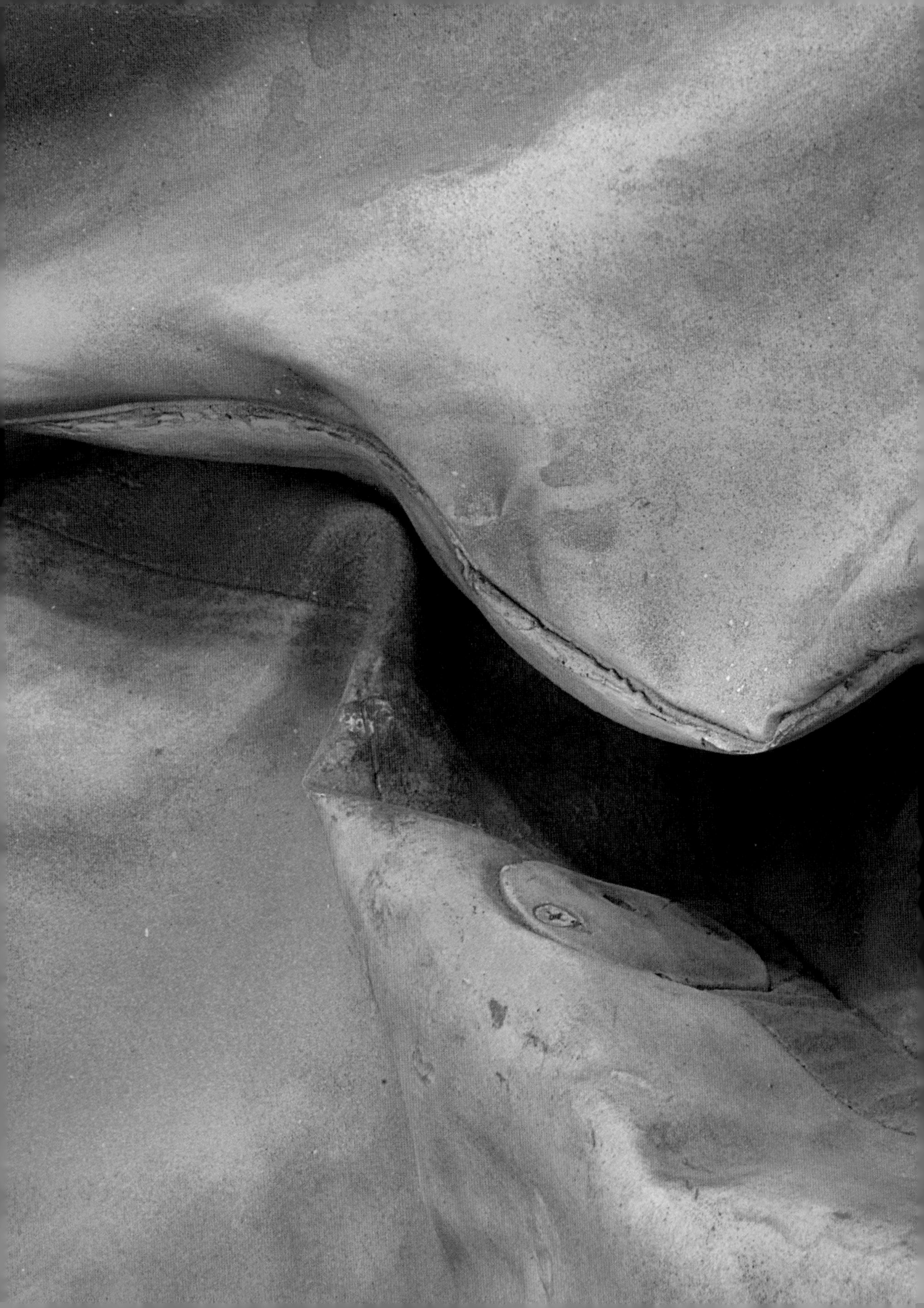

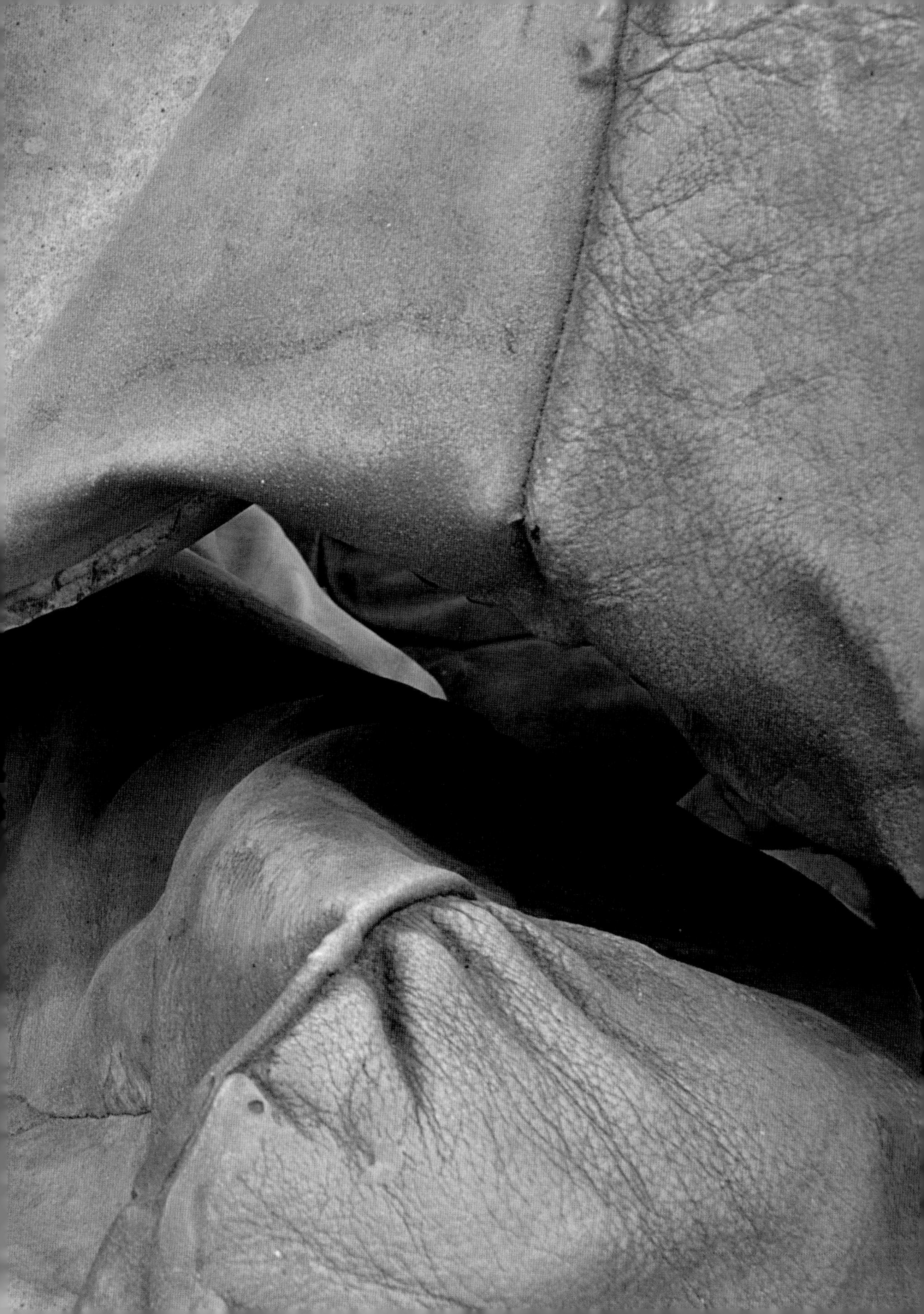

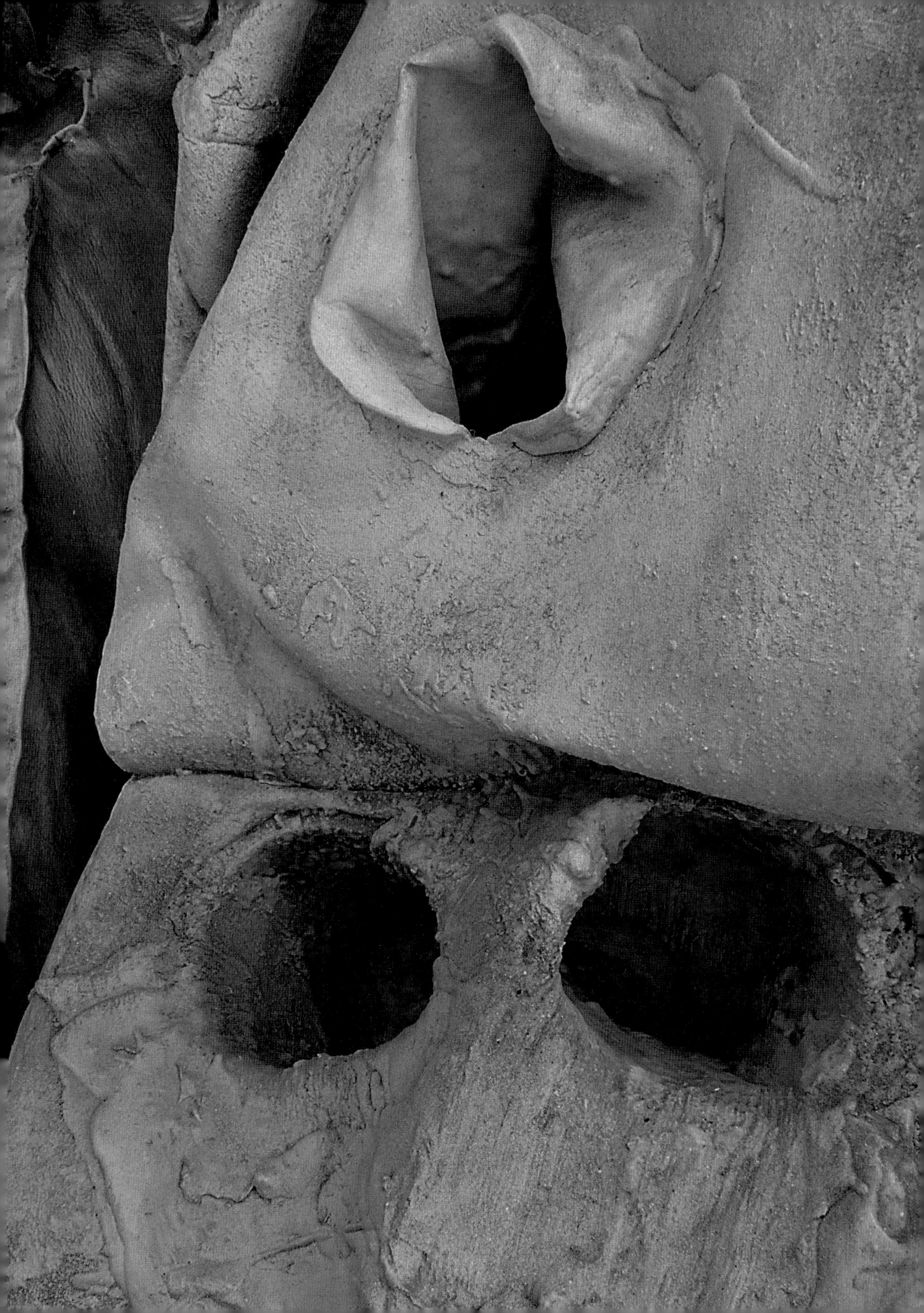

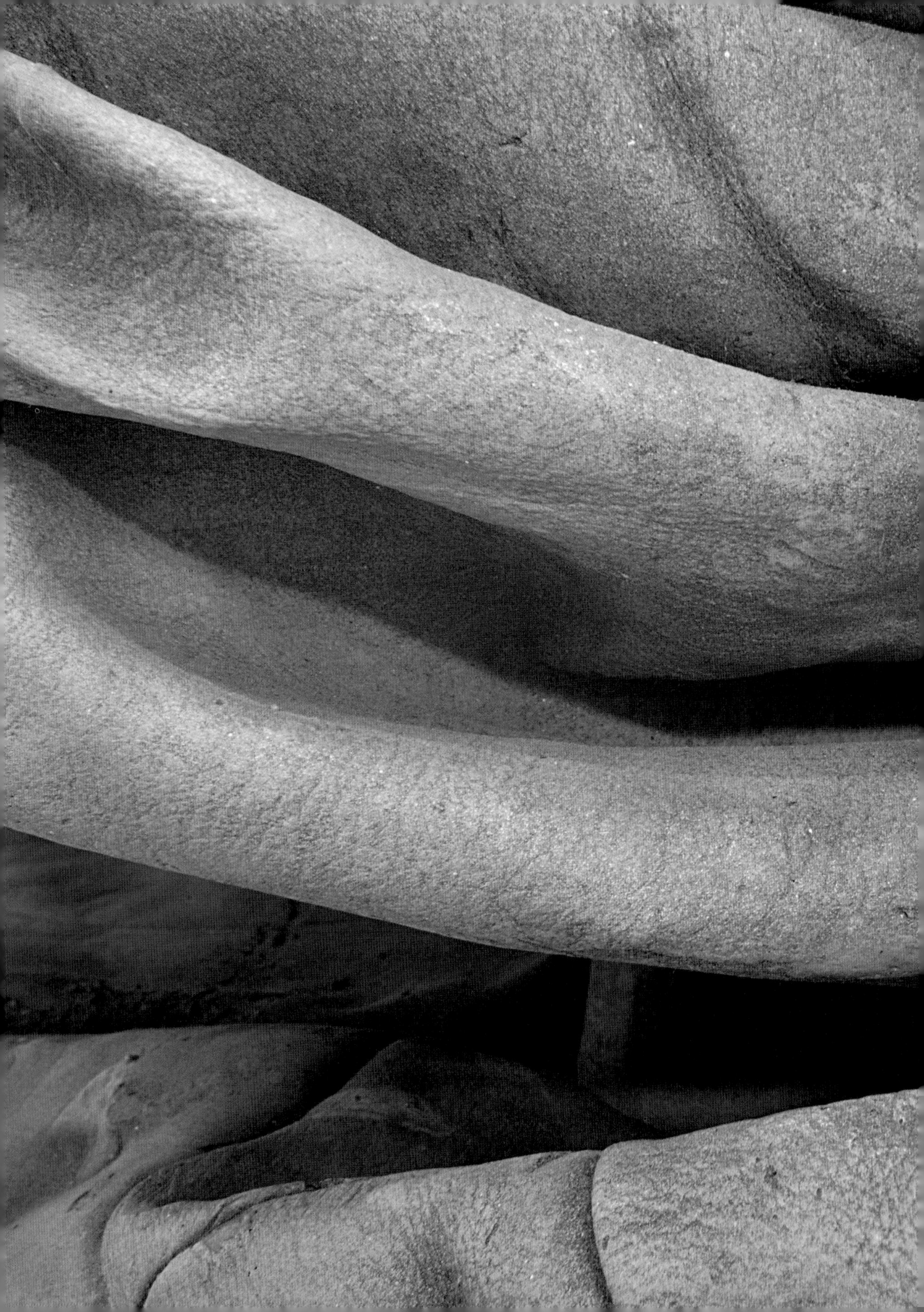

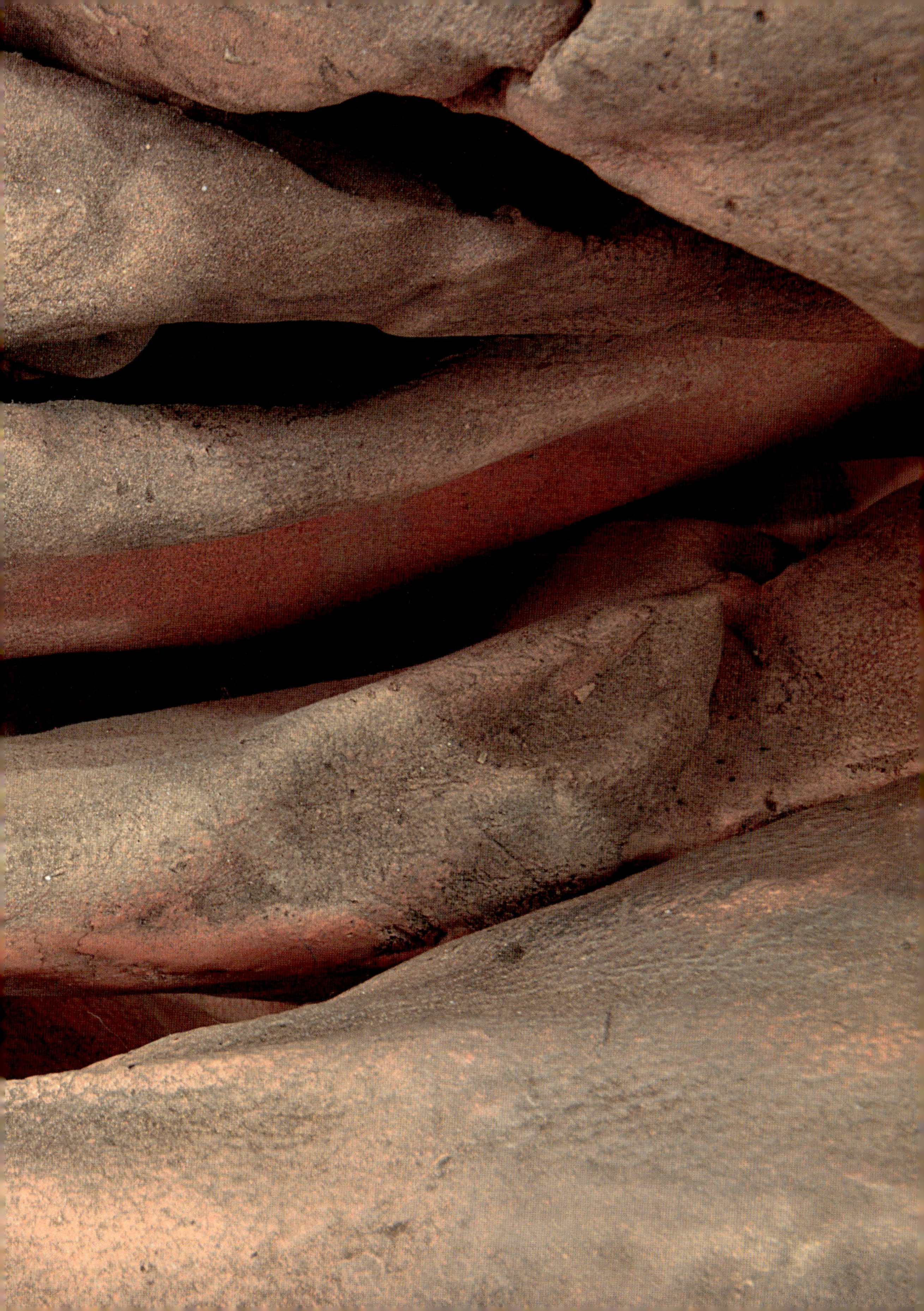

Costco–Imaginary Relationships, 2016–2017

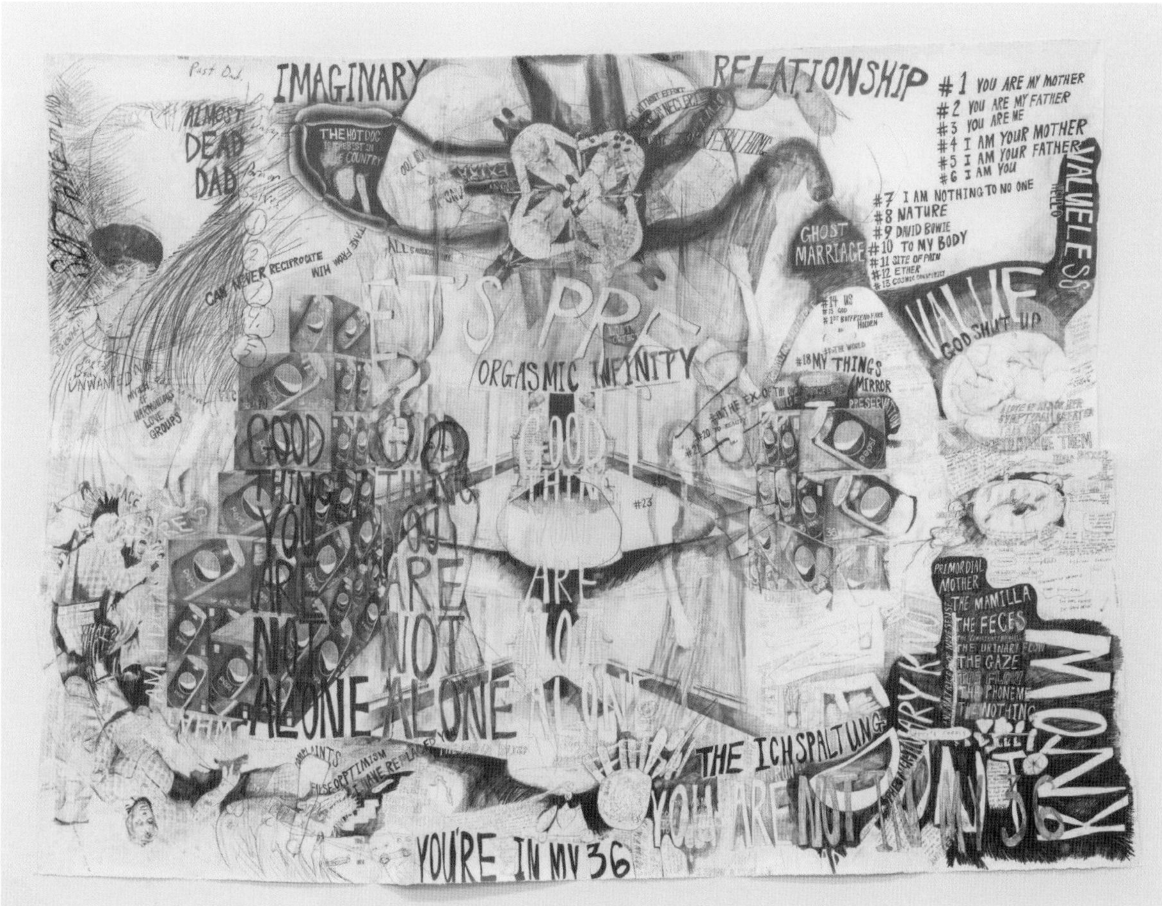

Past Dad.
IMAGINARY
RELATIONSHIP
#1 YOU ARE MY MOTHER
#2 YOU ARE MY FATHER
#3 YOU ARE ME
#4 I AM YOUR MOTHER
#5 I AM YOUR FATHER
#6 I AM YOU
#7 I AM NOTHING TO NO ONE
#8 NATURE
#9 DAVID BOWIE
#10 TO MY BODY
#11 SITE OF PAIN
#12 ETHER
ALMOST DEAD DAD
GHOST MARRIAGE
VALUELESS
VALUE
GOD SHUT UP
CAN NEVER RECIPROCATE
ORGASMIC INFINITY
#18 MY THINGS
MIRROR
GOOD THING YOU ARE NOT ALONE
GOOD THING YOU ARE NOT ALONE
PRIMORDIAL MOTHER
THE MAMILLA
THE FECES
THE GAZE
THE NOTHING
THE ICHSPALTUNG
YOU ARE NOT
YOU'RE IN MV 36

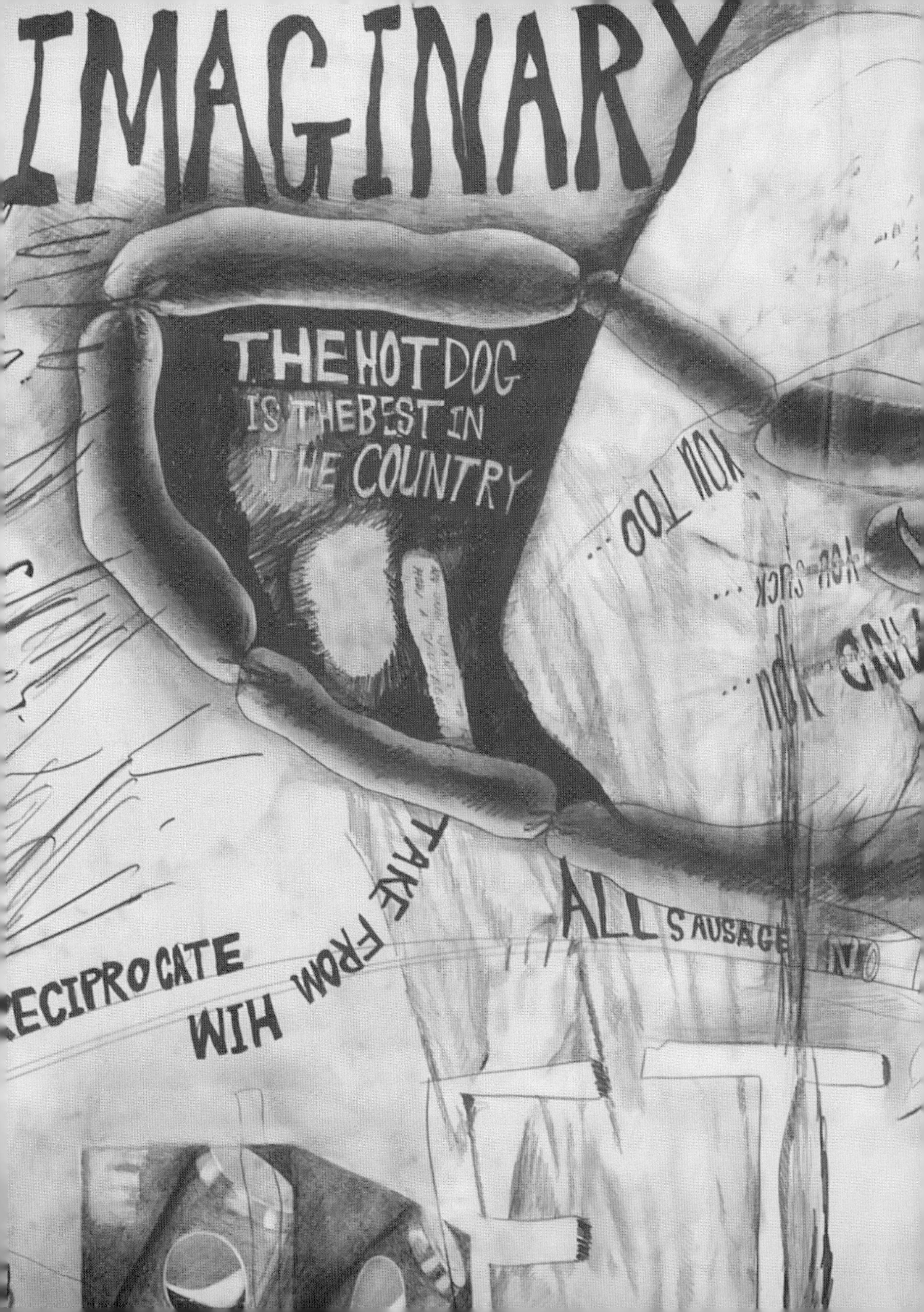

IMAGINARY
THE HOT DOG
IS THE BEST IN
THE COUNTRY
YOU TOO ...
YOU SUCK ...
AND you ...
TAKE FROM HIM
ALL SAUSAGE
RECIPROCATE

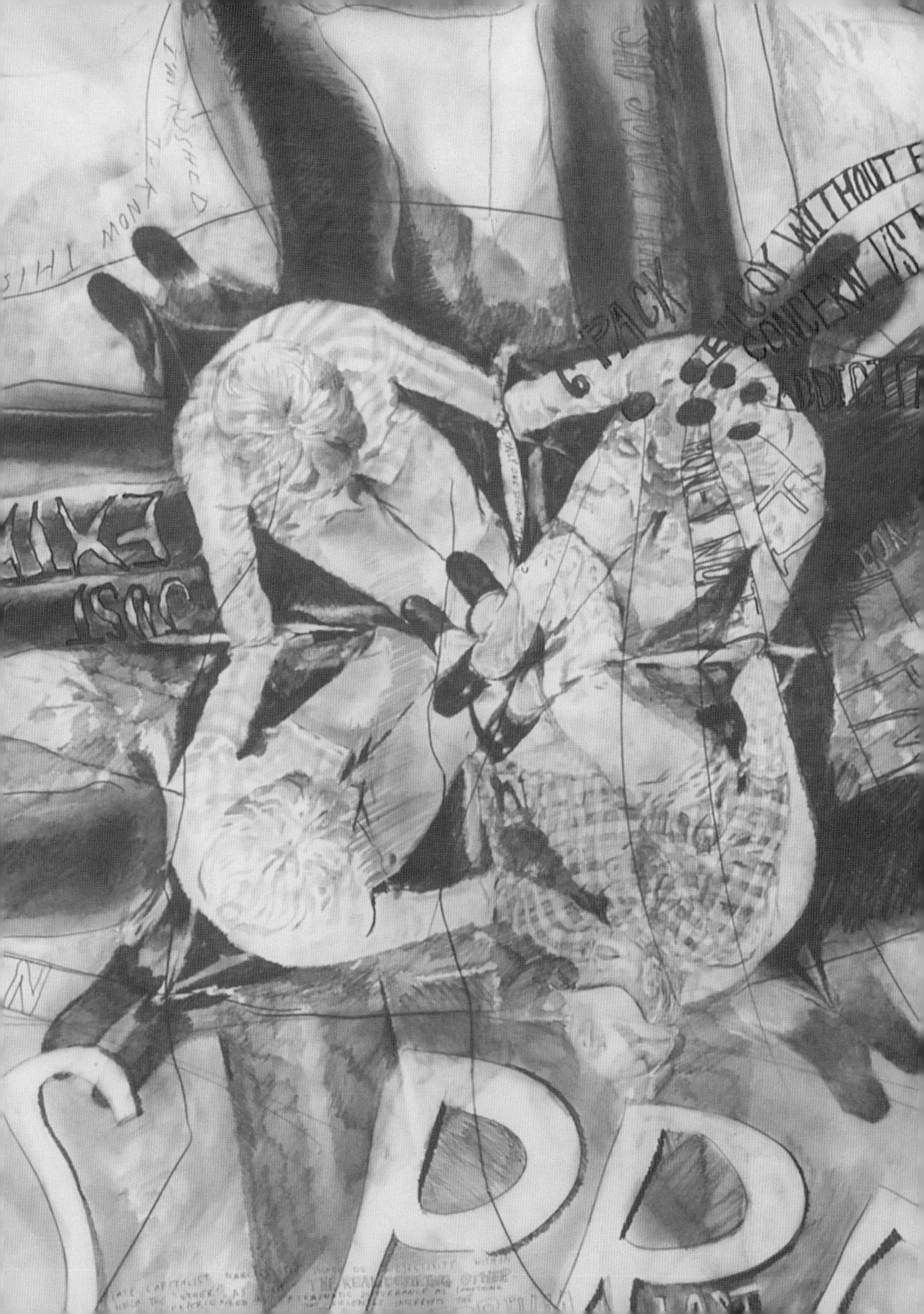
PACK
WITHOUT
CONCERN

Two Hers, 2017

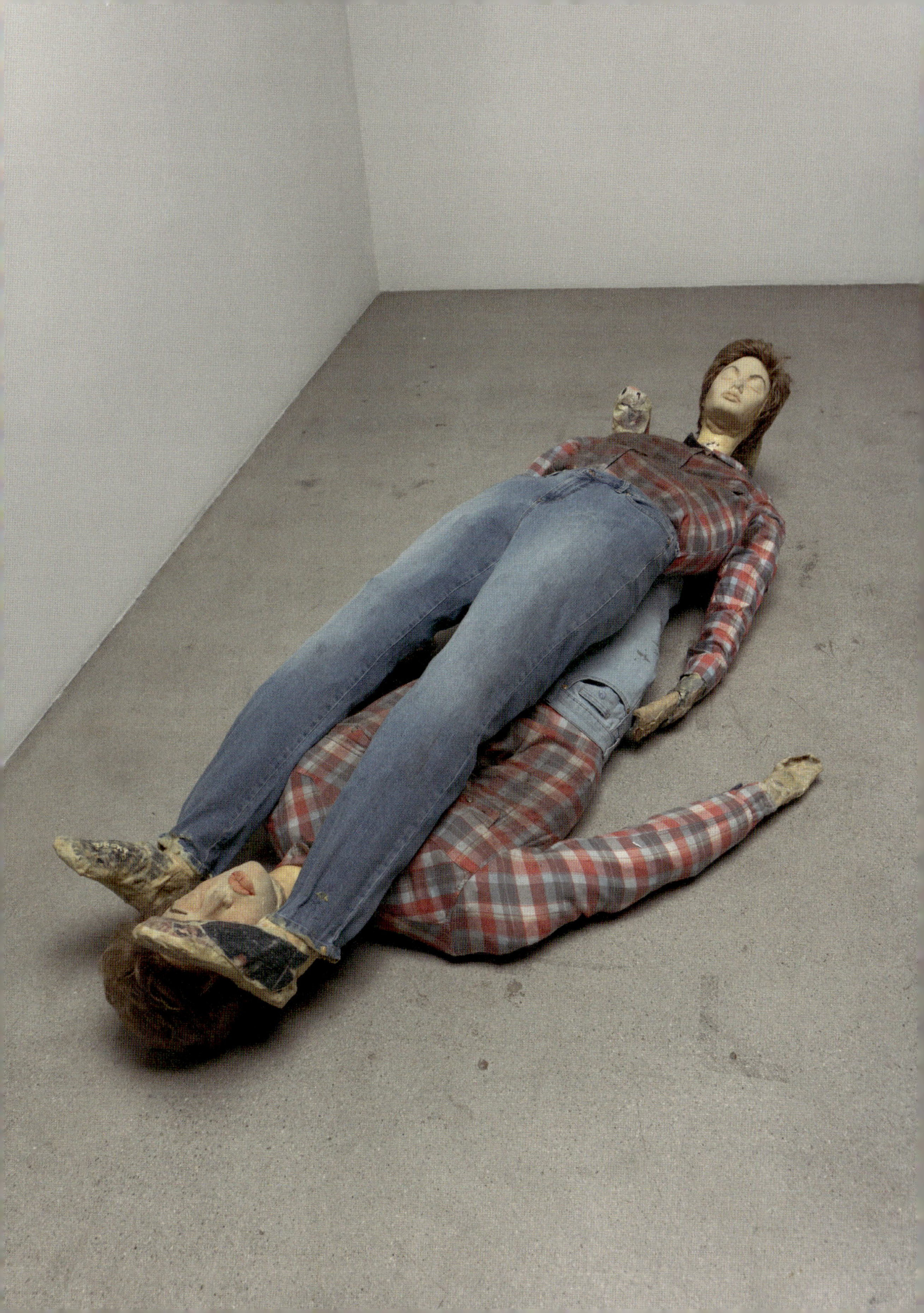

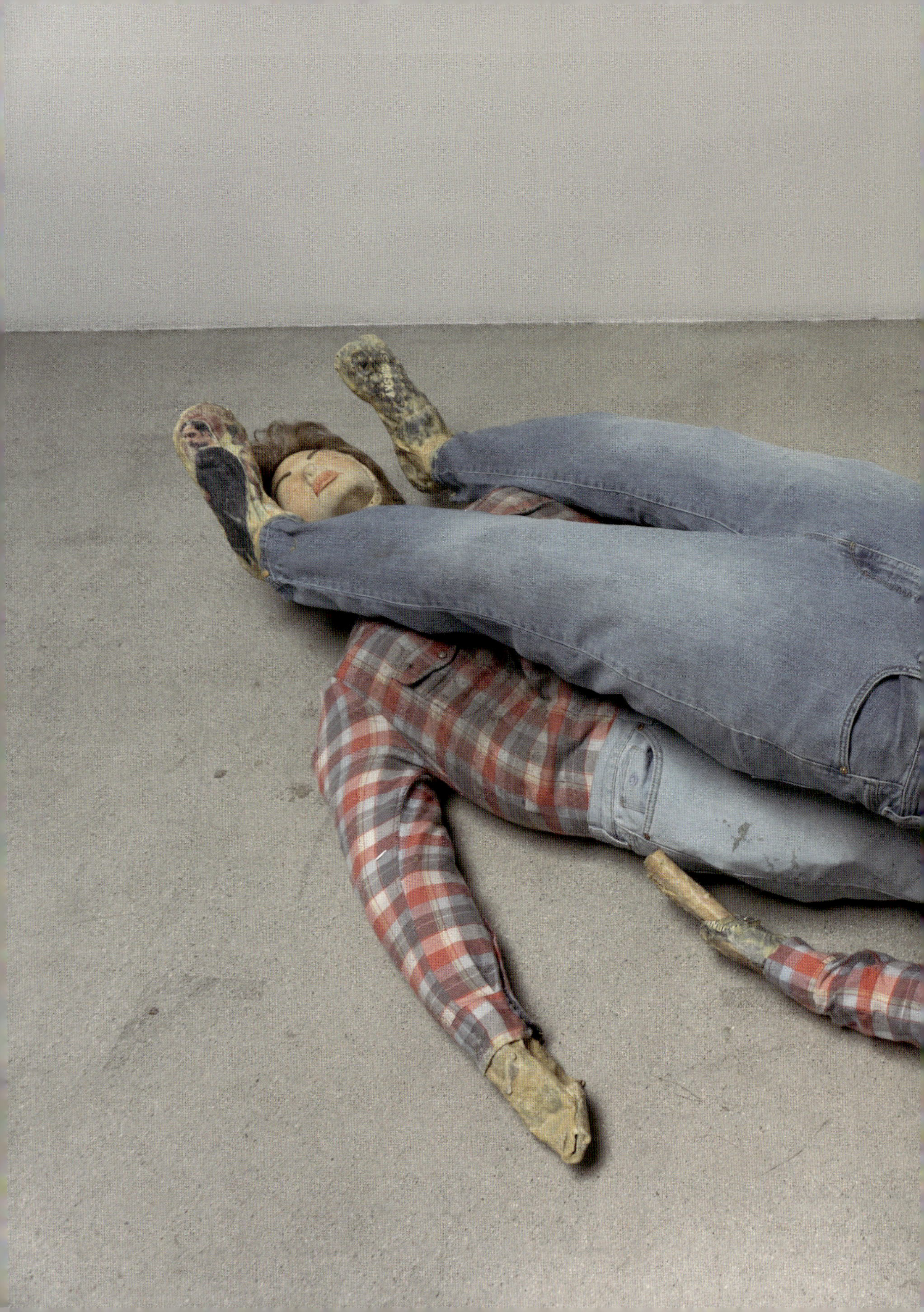

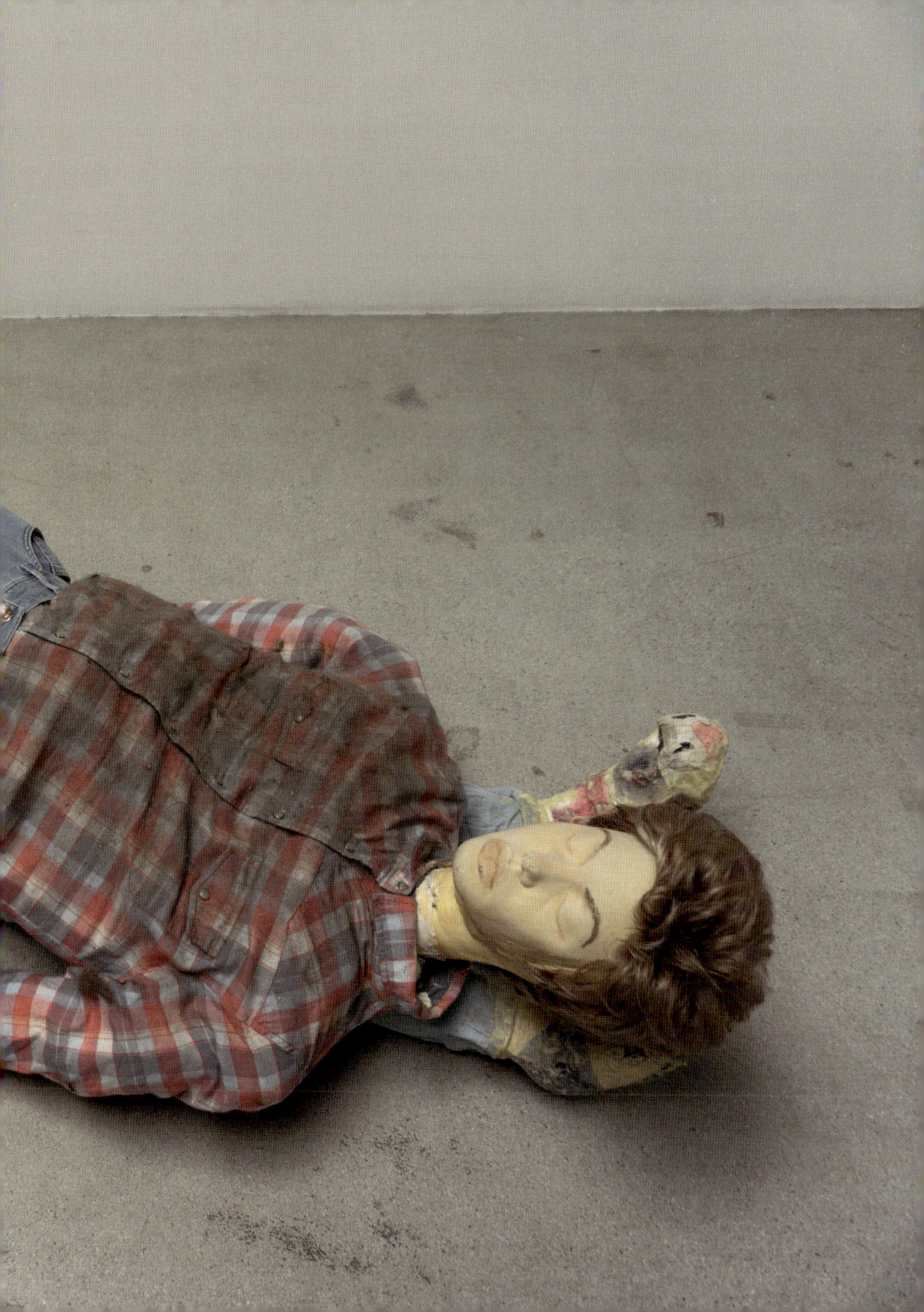

Mother Drain, 2017

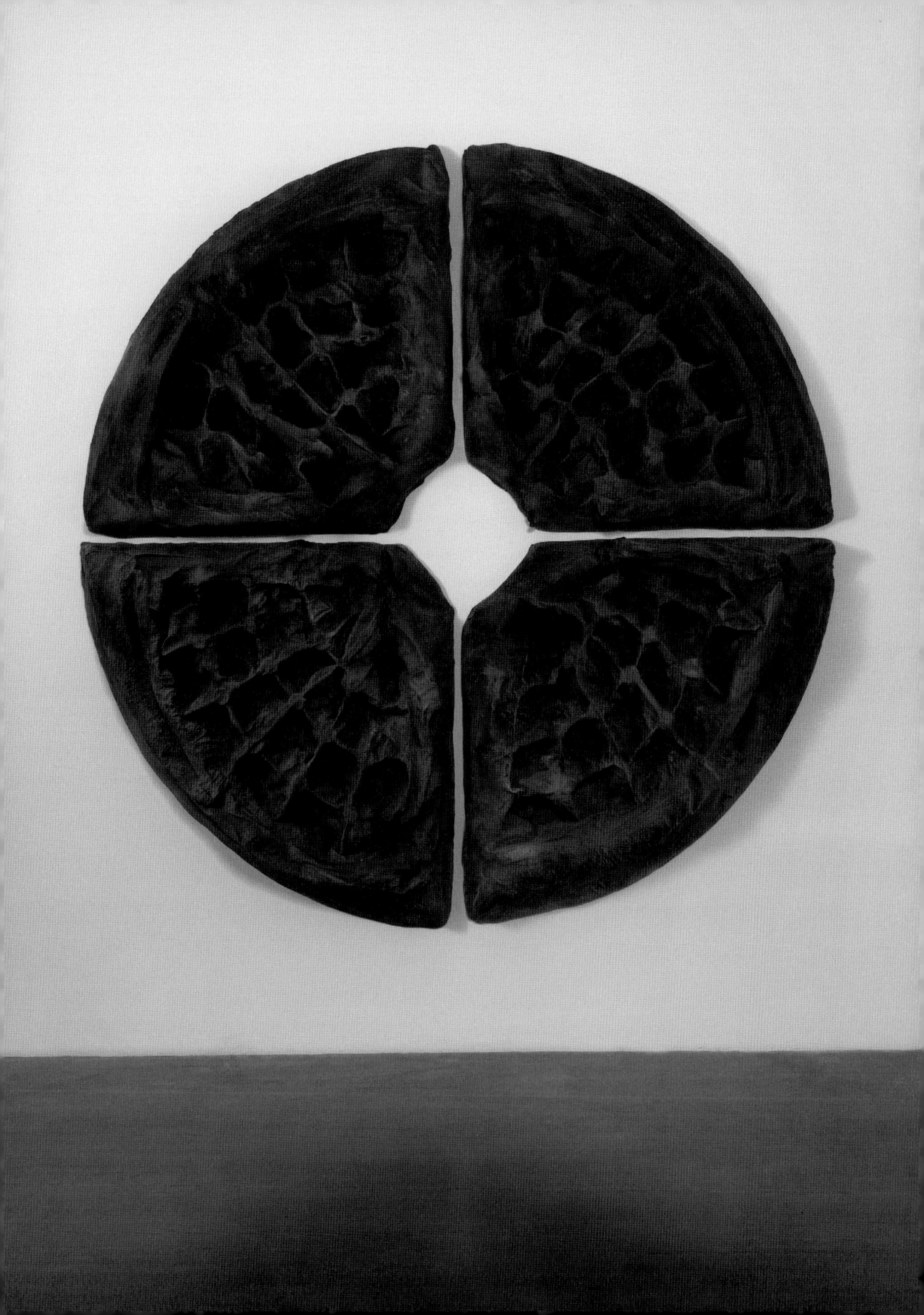

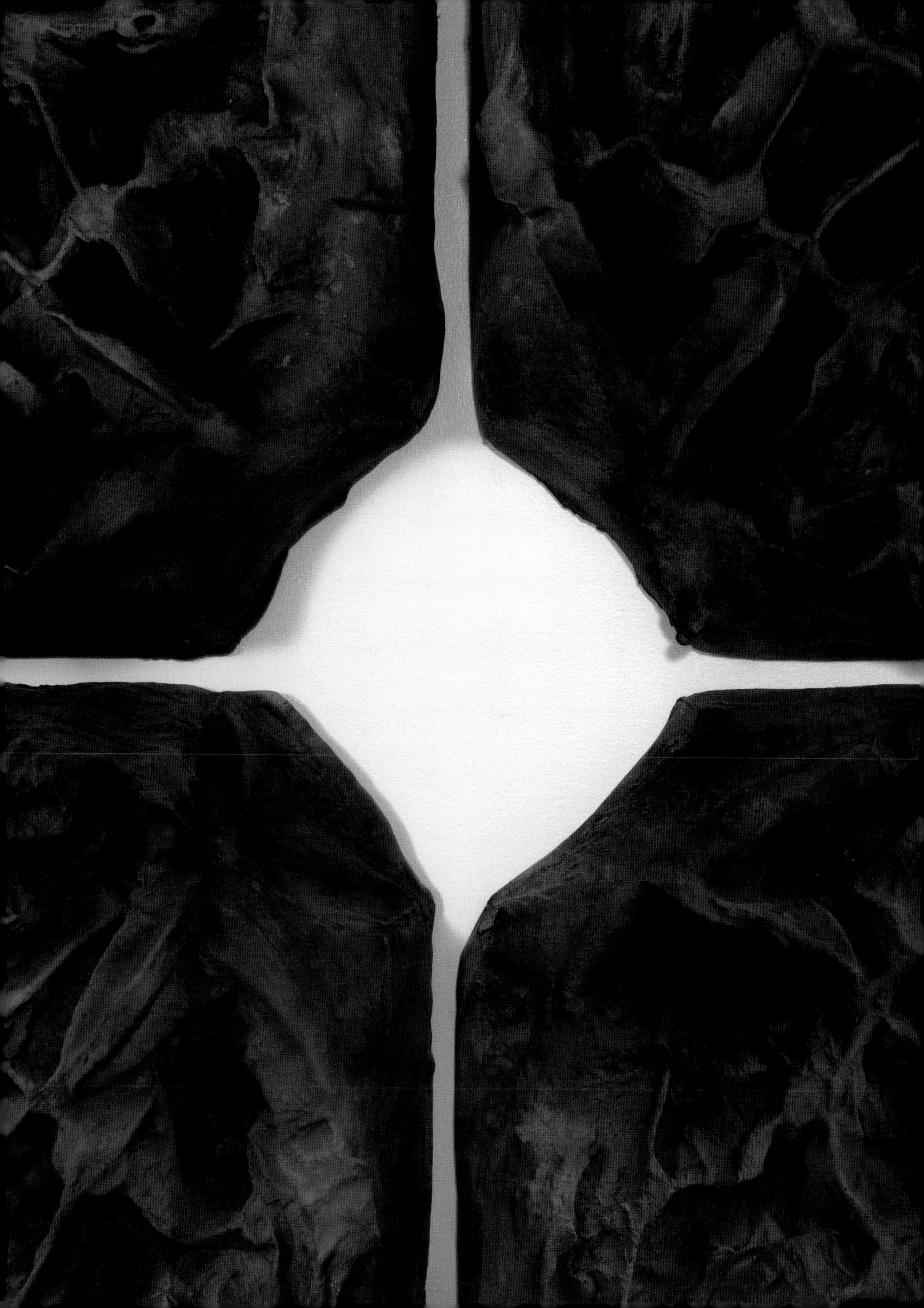

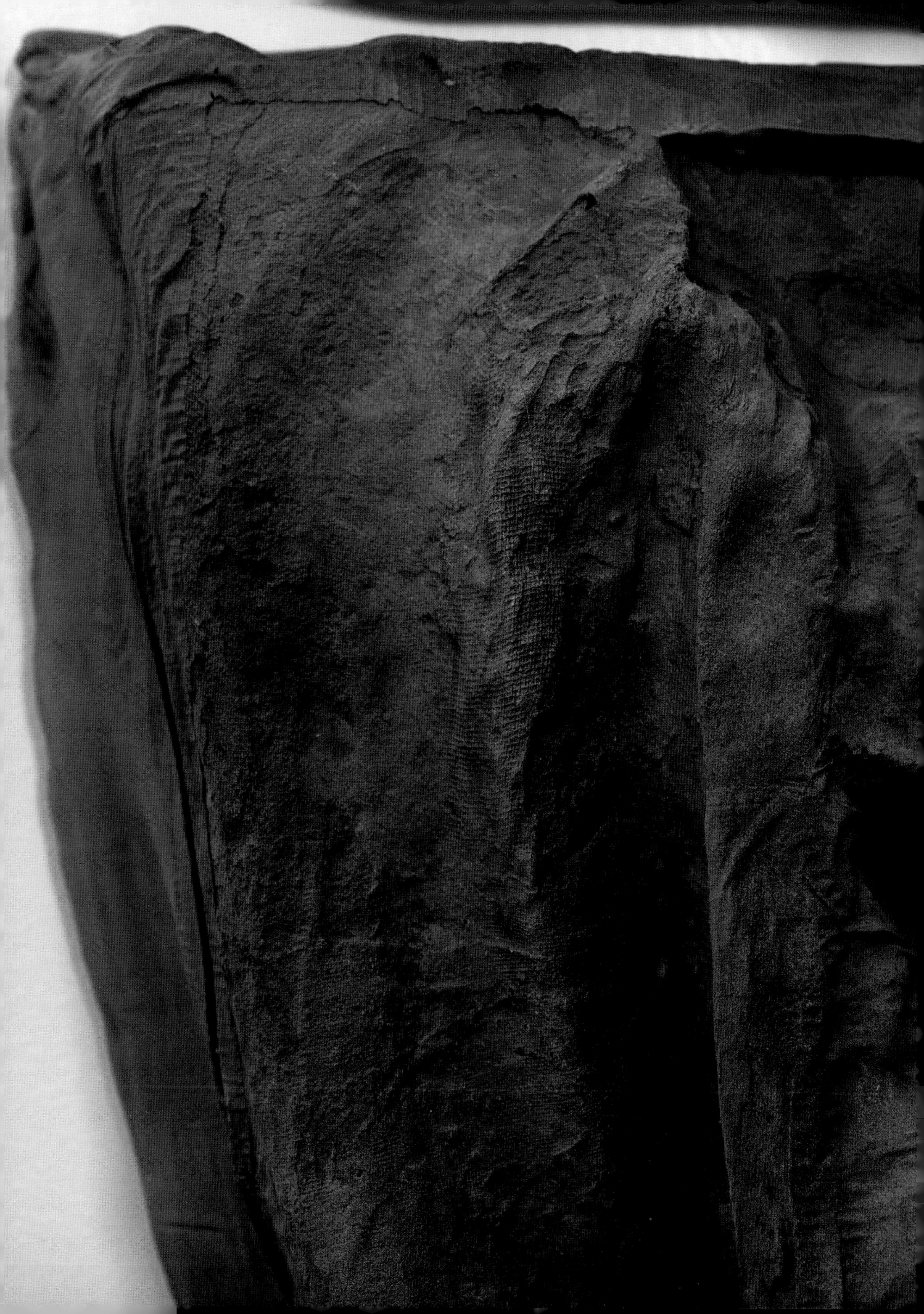

Big Tooth (Dream), 2017

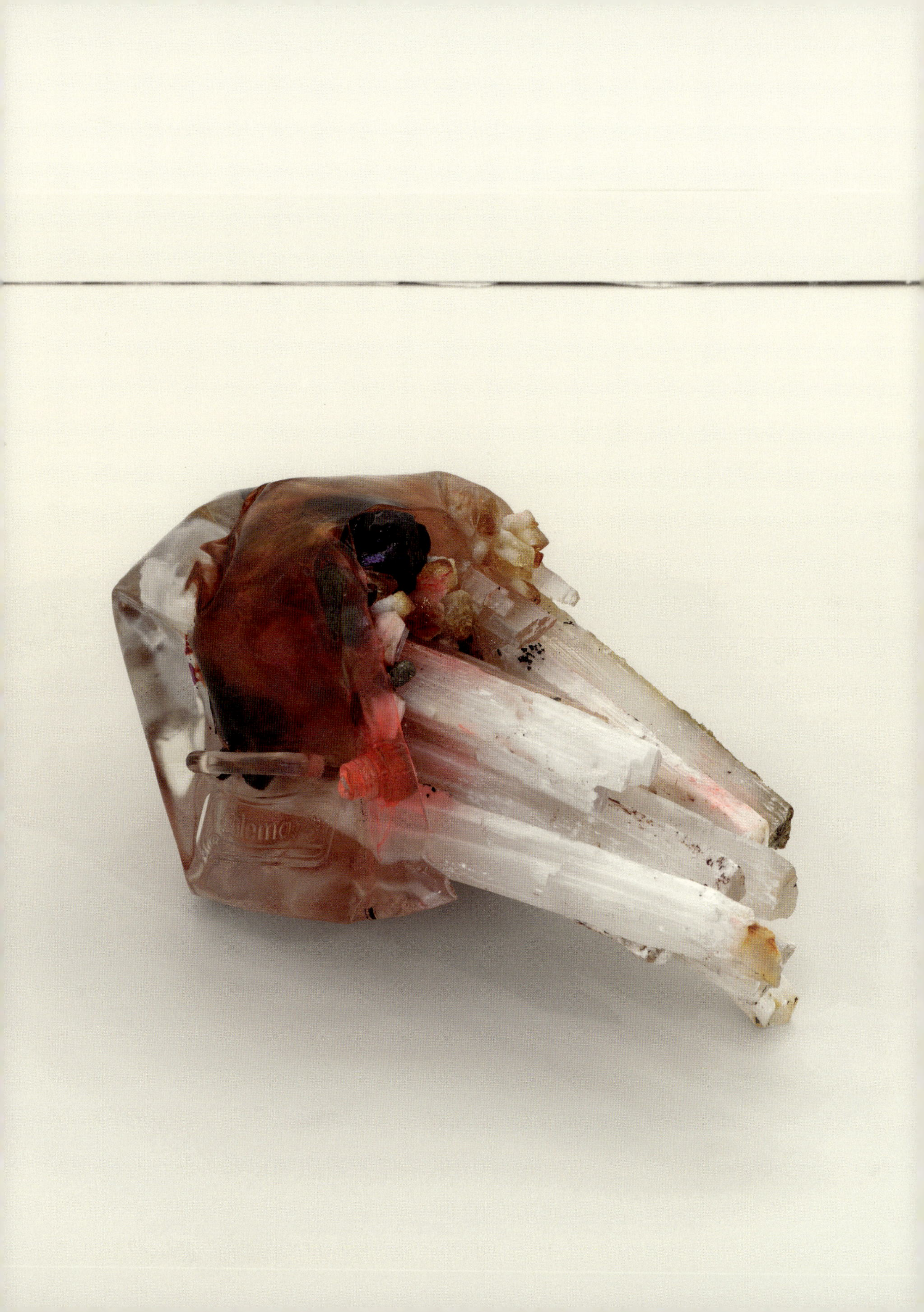

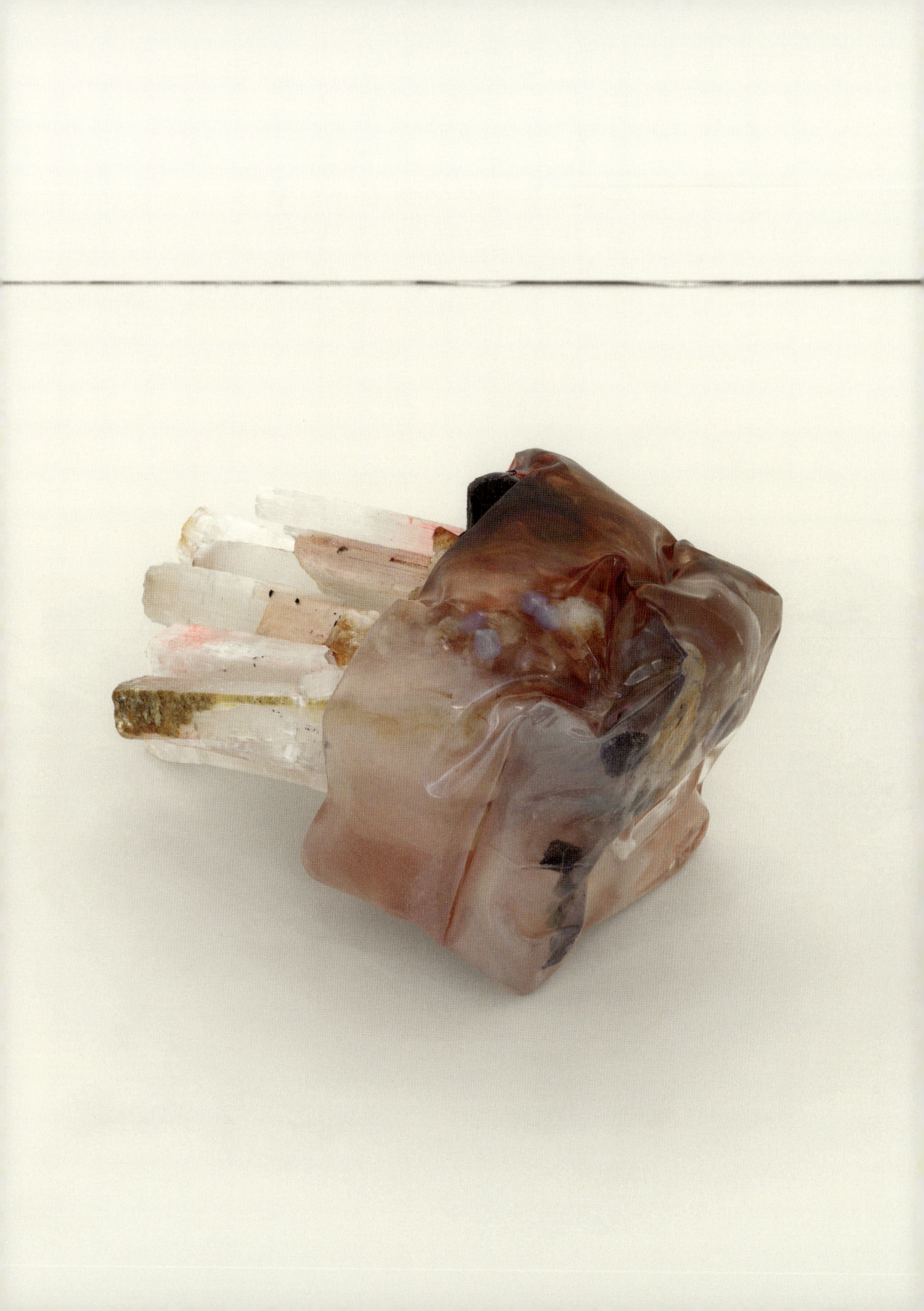

LIST OF WORKS

Untitled (Kiss), 2008
Oil on panel
Two parts, each 122 × 122 cm

Kiss Skinned 1, 2009
Oil on canvas
Two parts, each 50.8 × 50.8 cm

Event Horizon, 2011–2017
Graphite, ink, and gesso on paper
102.9 × 184.2 cm

Cult of Invalidism, 2012
Silicone, charcoal, dirt, hair
121.9 × 182.8 cm

End Is Where We Start From, 2013
Silicone, spandex, fiberglass
137.2 × 76.2 × 14 cm

226, 2013
Silicone
212 × 153 × 30 cm

192, 2013
Silicone
215 × 187 × 25 cm

Who's Afraid of Red, Yellow, and Blue, 2014
Urethane, pigment, aluminum
216.5 × 198 × 78 cm

Door (closet), 2014–2016
Urethane, pigment, aluminum, steel, gypsum
203.2 × 77.5 × 22.9 cm

Position 4.8, 2015
Urethane, pigment, aluminum
173 × 170.5 × 31 cm

Dismembered/Remembered (Charcoal Figures), 2015
Charcoal, wax, wood
Two parts, each 243.8 × 121.1 × 25.4 cm

Untitled (1000 cans), 2015
Aluminum
1000 cans, each 12.7 × 6.4 cm

Brown Recluse, 2015
Urethane, pigment, aluminum
228.6 × 91.5 × 83.8 cm

12:43 A.M., 2015
Watercolor and watercolor pencil on paper
mounted on aluminum panel
240 × 127 cm

Death Bed, 2015
Silicone, nylon, fiberglass
215.9 × 90.2 × 17.1 cm

Crib Diptych, 2015
Silicone, nylon, fiberglass
Two parts, each 96.5 × 61 × 12.7 cm

Left Brace Erase, Back Brace Face, 2016
Urethane, pigment, aluminum
Two parts, each 203.2 × 213.4 × 208.3 cm

Costco–Imaginary Relationships, 2016–2017
Graphite, ink, and gesso on paper
260.4 × 360.7 cm

Two Hers, 2017
Latex, synthetic hair, acrylic, *Artforum* pages,
fabric, foam, duct tape, cat hair, debris
Two parts, each 15.2 × 182.4 × 45.6 cm

Mother Drain, 2017
Urethane foam, aluminum, pigment
228.6 × 228.6 × 27.9 cm

Big Tooth (Dream), 2017
Crystal selenite-resin composite, aluminum shavings,
dirt, opalene, crystal quartz, black quartz, dye, copper
66 × 33 × 33 cm

ARTIST BIO

Kaari Upson was born in San Bernardino, California in 1972. She studied at California Institute of the Arts, where she received her BA in 2004 and her MFA in 2007. From her ongoing series, "The Larry Project," to her unique smoke paintings, sculptures, video installations, and paintings, Upson's willingness to experiment and her versatility as an object-maker allow her to transform everyday items into sacred and profane relics that explore the psychology of the self and the effects of trauma, memory, and obsession on the individual.

Upson has exhibited in numerous institutions around the world, with solo shows at, among others: New Museum, New York (2017); SITE Santa Fe, Santa Fe (2010); Hammer Museum, Los Angeles (2007–2008); and California Institute of the Arts, Valencia (2007). Her work has been included in the group shows *Los Angeles – A Fiction*, Astrup Fearnley Museet, Oslo (2016); *Sleepless: The Bed in History and Contemporary Art*, 21er Haus, Vienna (2015); *Second Chances*, Aspen Art Museum, Aspen, Colorado (2015); *Procession*, CAPC Musée d'art contemporain, Bordeaux (2014); *The Los Angeles Project*, Ullens Center for Contemporary Art (UCCA), Beijing; *Inner Journeys*, Maison Particulière, Brussels (2013); *Test Pattern*, Whitney Museum of American Art, New York (2013); *The Residue of Memory*, Aspen Art Museum, Aspen, Colorado (2012); *American Exuberance*, Rubell Family Collection, Miami (2011); *George Herms: Xenophilia (Love of the Unknown)*, MOCA Pacific Design Center, Los Angeles (2011); *Involuntary*, Ford Project, New York (2011); *Nine Lives: Visionary Artists from L.A.*, Hammer Museum, Los Angeles (2009); and *SACK OF BONES*, Peres Projects, Los Angeles (2008). Upson lives and works in Los Angeles.

AUTHOR BIO

Ali Subotnick is an independent curator and adjunct curator at the Hammer Museum in Los Angeles, where she has organized numerous exhibitions including *UH-OH: Frances Stark 1991–2015* (2015); *LLYN FOULKES* (2013); *The Afghan Carpet Project* (2015); *JG, a film by Tacita Dean* (2013–2014); *Mark Leckey: On Pleasure Bent* (2013); *Made in L.A. 2012* (cocurated with the Hammer's Anne Ellegood and in collaboration with LAXART), and the accompanying *Venice Beach Biennial*; *Nine Lives: Visionary Artists from L.A.* (2009); *Richard Hawkins: Third Mind*, the traveling exhibition originally curated by Lisa Dorin for The Art Institute of Chicago (2011); and *The Bible Illuminated: R. Crumb's Book of Genesis* (2010). At the Hammer Museum, Subotnick has curated debut American museum exhibitions for artists such as Yuri Ancarani, Neïl Beloufa, Erin Cosgrove, Roberto Cuoghi, Nathalie Djurberg, Julian Hoeber, Jamie Isenstein, Erik van Lieshout, Nathaniel Mellors, Stephen G. Rhodes, and Andra Ursuta, as well as Kaari Upson.

In 2006, along with Maurizio Cattelan and Massimiliano Gioni, she cocurated *Of Mice and Men*, the 4th Berlin Biennial for Contemporary Art. Other collaborations with Cattelan and Gioni include the creation of The Wrong Gallery (2002) and *Charley* magazine (2000). She has written about art and culture for *Frieze*, *Parkett*, *ARTnews*, and *ArtReview*, among other publications, and was the contributor to *Roberto Cuoghi: 2000 Words*.

It was through the Wrong Gallery that I first learned about Kaari Upson. It never showed her, but its three founders played an essential role in acquainting me with her work: Maurizio Cattelan introduced me to her, Massimiliano Gioni encouraged me to delve further, and Ali Subotnick took me to her studio in LA. Ever since I got to know Kaari, I have been obsessed by her haunting sculptures. Her commitment to her art reminds me of a prizefighter's fierce determination. My sincere thanks must go first to Kaari. Many thanks to Ali, not only for bringing me to her studio but for her illuminating essay. My deepest gratitude to Massimiliano and Karen Marta for their ongoing commitment to bringing the 2000 Words series to life. And finally, to Brendan Dugan for his enduring design concept and to Sue Medlicott for ensuring that the production is always at the highest level.

—Dakis Joannou

Kaari Upson
2000 Words

Commissioning Editor: Massimiliano Gioni
Editor: Karen Marta
Design concept and cover: An Art Service
Managing Editor: Tommaso Speretta
Line Editor: Christopher Impiglia
Project Manager: Regina Alivisatos
Registrar: Natasha Polymeropoulos
Copy Editor: Nausicaa Renner
Proofreader: Kyra Sutton
Production: The Production Department

Published by:
Fondation DESTE pour l'art Contemporain
22, Henri Mussard
1208 Geneva, Switzerland
www.deste.gr

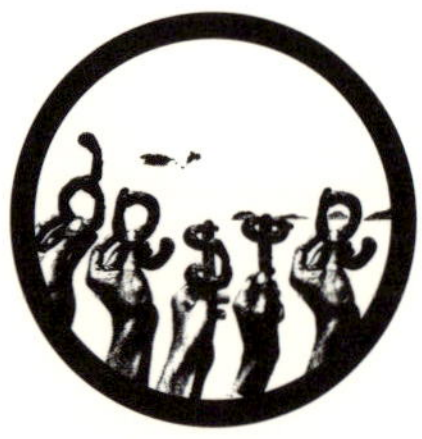